THE POWER OF
ONE

Adventures in rediscovering the unity of the Spirit

TIM ROBERTS

RIVER
PUBLISHING

River Publishing & Media Ltd
Barham Court
Teston
Maidstone
Kent
ME18 5BZ
United Kingdom

info@river-publishing.co.uk

Copyright © Tim Roberts 2015

All rights reserved. No part of this publication may be reproduced, stored in a retrieval system, or transmitted in any form or by any means, electronic, mechanical, photocopying or otherwise, without the prior written consent of the publisher. Short extracts may be used for review purposes.

Holy Bible. New Living Translation copyright© 1996, 2004, 2007, 2013 by Tyndale House Foundation. Used by permission of Tyndale House Publishers Inc., Carol Stream, Illinois 60188. All rights reserved.

ISBN 978-1-908393-50-0
Cover design by www.spiffingcovers.com
Printed in the United Kingdom
Printed by Bell & Bain Ltd, Glasgow

Contents

What Others Are Saying About This Book...

"Through the years I have watched first hand Tim Roberts – a man of the Spirit and a peacemaker – live his life loving people and leading his family and congregation in practicing what he has written in this book. I commend this book to you. This is such an essential foundation for the proper development of an individual, a family and a church, if there is to be healthy relationships and partnerships. I look forward to witnessing the testimonies of those whose lives will be changed by reading it and, in a more profound way, enjoying the unity of the Spirit."

Ron Corzine
Christian Fellowship International, San Antonio, Texas

"Christ's prayer '...that they might be One' (John 17:21), is possibly one of the most important utterances ever spoken by Jesus. Tim Roberts has a tremendous understanding of what is contained in that statement and systematically takes the reader on an important and practical journey of discovery in relation to the power of unity. All will be challenged and blessed by this excellent call for Christians to not just talk of unity, but actually practice it. I recommend it unreservedly to everyone serious about living as Christ commands and embracing the Power of One."

John Partington
National Leader Assemblies of God GB

"Tim Roberts provides a very compelling message on the centrality of unity to impact cities. Tim is both a pastor and a practitioner in city movements. This is an important read."

Dr Mac Pier
CEO, The NYC Leadership Center
Senior Associate for Cities, Lausanne

"Tim Roberts provides thought-provoking insights into the idea of unity. This often-talked about idea needs a fresh perspective, which Tim gives with grace and wisdom. Especially helpful is Tim's practical guidance for leaders in developing greater unity among their team. *The Power of One* will greatly help you understand and lead your team, whether in business or church, into a greater dimension of unity."

Joel Holm
Church/Missions Consultant, formerly of Willow Creek

"I have known Tim for many years and in that time I've witnessed two consistent values he lives by, namely those of integrity and generosity. At the same time, I've experienced two of his greatest passions, namely his love for the Church and his love for a lost world. As I read this book I hear my friend and feel his heart bleed on every page. I'm privileged to know the author and so it is with absolute confidence that I can assure you that what you are about to read is not the musings of a man writing about some random topic. Rather, Tim is in every word, on every page. Tim's message of unity comes from a life spent working towards it. Let his integrity and generosity of spirit infect you. Let his love for the Church and God's world inspire you. God is one and He calls His people to be one also."

Dr John Andrews
Principal, Mattersey Hall

Dedication

This book is dedicated to my best friend, partner for life and the one with whom I am most joyfully united, Helen: love you, babe! Also to Bethany, Hannah and David, three Incredibles who are destined to change their world: love you so much and I am so glad to be your dad!

Foreword

All over the world and all around this country a new spirit of unity is breaking out across the Church of Christ. Something very significant has been happening under the radar and hidden away. God has been doing a work behind the scenes in villages, towns and cities across the nation. This is not manufactured, copied, hyped or simply the latest fashionable thing to do. It is a work of the Spirit because it cuts against human nature and challenges our need often to be independent, selfish and insular.

All over the country church leaders, leaders of Christian agencies and Christian leaders in society, are laying down their own agendas and differences to become friends, to pray together and work together for the sake of blessing the places they have been sent to serve. From Sydney to Newcastle, from Portland to Plymouth, from Indonesia to Brazil, in cities and towns all over the globe, God has been building together an expression of Jesus' prayer in John 17: *"That they may be one ... so that the world may believe."*

From this platform of a growing unity, people are beginning to lift up their eyes towards a greater vision of prayer and working for the transformation of their town or city; to believe that in two or three decades the place they live in could be substantially improved, culturally, socially and spiritually.

This unity isn't only being expressed among local church leaders and Christian charities, it also beginning to form across cultural spheres. Christians in business from different locations are beginning to connect and support each other, praying together for greater kingdom strategic alignment. Christians in the arts are forming close, prayerful friendships across cities and towns, with a vision to see the cultural context blessed with Shalom, resulting in more beautiful places, events, celebrations and exhibitions that reflect the Creator of the cosmos. Educationalists who love Christ and seek to be a faithful witness are creating contexts for support, inspiration and strategic action. This coming together of the Church in its widest sense is happening right across all the other spheres, such as in the media, sport, civic life, politics, family life and other areas.

Gather (www.wegather.co.uk) based here in the UK has been tracking this move of God across the nation and linking with other networks across all five continents. "Christians Across Watford" is one of the most mature and experienced unity-for-transformation movements in the country. Tim Roberts and others have led this unity movement with great dedication, commitment and passion for many years.

This book is, on the one hand, an excellent biblical argument for the cause of unity to be pursued with renewed vigor. But it is also, at a much deeper level, a lived theology of unity.

The biblical truths Tim highlights have been lived out over many years during the everyday task of maintaining greater unity across Watford. When Tim focuses on the biblical challenge of humility, generosity, maturity and tenacity he is not simply underlining some key words in a passage, he is speaking with deep experience and often some pain. When he talks about the challenges of diversity, harmony and dignity he speaks through lived experience.

As I read this book I was struck again by the sheer weight of the biblical mandate towards unity emanating from the nature of the Triune God. With such core teaching we are left to wonder why this has become such a blindspot in many sections of the Church. Why so often do our inter-church relationships become at best bland and at worst competitive? Why are so many churches more interested in protecting their own brand, doing their own thing and building their own empire?

This book fundamentally challenges this self-centered approach to ministry and inspires us to worship God in expressing one of his most beautiful characteristics. When the beauty of unity is seen then the world will know that Christ is Lord.

This book will be one of the first among many to come out of the developing unity movements across the world. A new library will be created documenting, theologising and highlighting this move of the Spirit in our day. I am very thankful to Tim Roberts for adding to this collection of much needed material. I hope you will be inspired, challenged and motivated to either begin to work for unity, or continue to press on with what you are doing, in your village, town, borough or city.

Rev Roger Sutton
Director of Gather www.wegather.co.uk
Co-director of Every Place www.every-place.co.uk

Preface

In the same way that love is, unity is a glorious end in itself. Perfect unity is the very nature of God and, as followers of Christ, we look ahead to the unified worship of all creation in heaven as our ultimate destination. This book is written as a travel guide towards that terminus which is, of course, not the end, but a new and eternal beginning. As with other travel guides, this work is the product of my own experiences along the way interwoven with other people's thoughts, experiences, writings and creations, some of which I have diligently cross-referenced and others I give general credit to now. I am indebted to the scholars and thinkers, the friends and colleagues, who have added fuel to this fire within; this unquenchable passion I have been given for the Church to live in greater unity.

My beautiful, faithful wife, Helen, is also my best friend and the ultimate co-pilot in our family's mission. She has continually spurred me on to spread this fiery battle against division and I am grateful to her, our children and the Wellspring Church family for their generous, prayerful support to give time and space in pursuit of this project.

As I sit here overlooking the River Thames, I also want to acknowledge Helen's parents for providing a peaceful bolt-hold to put these words in order. For all those who have made a contribution, many thanks to you; and all glory to the One who unites us.

The fruit of these next few chapters may simply be more thoughts, more questions, more wonderings, and an emerging awareness. I don't have lots of answers. Some say you learn more through writing than reading, so I'll be learning with you all the way. Philosopher Karl Popper admitted, *"No book can ever be finished. While working on it we learn just enough to find it immature the moment we turn away from it."*

Be that as it may, however immature this book, perhaps it will leave us chewing on food for our souls, strategies for our churches, wisdom that will help us grow and mature into the people, the leaders, He wants us to become.

What I do hope you glean from this journey of discovery is that God is at work today uniting his people. There are profound signs of hope and encouragement that the Spirit of unity is moving us, even in the fragmented West, together in Christ, to a heavenly destination. As we set put out to sea, let's leave cynicism back in the harbour and stretch our sails to embrace the wind of God's Spirit. May he lead us in the ways everlasting. Thanks for jumping on board. This voyage wouldn't be the same without you.

Introduction:
Something Strange is Going On Here

The winter sun was streaming in between the blinds of a conference room as church leaders had gathered for a two-day retreat. Sitting, perhaps a little awkwardly, were leaders from across the broadest spectrum of churchmanship. The moment was latent with potential. There was the potential for a waste of precious time, the potential for a few doctrinal arguments, the potential for hiddenness and superficiality (yes, even church leaders fall prey to such things in moments of insecurity. Sorry to shock you).

But instead, the Spirit of God took over, and willing hearts were changed. I don't think we'll ever be the same.

Maybe the barriers of division began to fall during the first testimony: a respected Anglican leader opening up about how the last 6 months had really been for him; how he felt like packing it all in; how retirement couldn't come soon enough. He was so honest – and at a level that kicked pretence out of the window from the outset. Then a Catholic grandparent shared tearfully about the miraculous delivery of an ectopic child, the heavenly response to an "impossible" situation. Miracles? In a church where they don't always speak in tongues? What's going on?! As he shared, tear ducts were being loosened and the Spirit of unity began to move. It was strange. Wonderfully, beautifully strange.

In that same opening session, as people shared their perspectives and where they were at, a Quaker representative said how she felt "a strong urging" to come on this retreat. She had wondered if she'd be genuinely welcome and also wondered if it was a Quaker thing to participate in. To be honest, I wondered too. I was surprised to see her there. How broad could this gathering be and still have Christ-centred meaning? How did God feel about her being there and would he bless our retreat if we compromised too far?

The sun was setting but the retreat was gaining in intensity. Baptists and Charismatics were sharing how hard leadership can be and the need for more energy, more time, more finances, more strength, more young people in our churches, more grace and faith to keep going. The Catholics agreed and so did I; our burdens shared. The Seventh Day Adventist leaders, attending such a gathering for the first time, had also wondered what to expect and if they should be there. Their hearts opened, resonating with others' weariness and the load of leading others into faith. One of them had decided from the outset he wouldn't share honestly the darkness of soul he was experiencing, that is until others had so destroyed the dividing barriers between us that in the Spirit of unity, he couldn't hide. You could just feel the weight of God's presence in the room. I don't mean an overbearing heaviness, it was like the soft light of the candle on the table in the centre of the room, but burning equally, strongly within us all. This had gone from a Church Leaders Anonymous meeting into a deep encounter with the Spirit of God who was uniting us.

Over those hours of sharing, laughing, praying, thinking, reading, reflecting and eating together something strange was happening. This togetherness was on a new level. Even as I tell you, I am stirred with emotion, because I believe what we experienced is central to what God is doing in our nation, and the nations. This book is about that heavenly call.

Perhaps the pinnacle of this leaders' retreat for me was a moment almost too sacred, too profound to try and explain. But I will try. The last session before we headed back home was communion. I'd been asked to lead this and felt strongly that given where God had been leading us, we should all introduce communion. Dangerous in a room of nearly twenty ministers and preachers – we didn't have five hours! Each of us took turns to share about the Lord's Table and what this meal meant to us, personally and (inevitably) within our denominational tradition.

It was confounding, startling, inspiring and convicting. One Catholic priest apologised for the way his branch of the Church had claimed a monopoly on this meal. For him it was a simple meal, available to all who called on the name of Christ. He was happy to share this bread and this cup with everyone else in the room. Others concurred. We all come to the cross of Jesus as sinners who needed saving. Each of us have been saved by the free gift of God's grace and what unites us is our childlike confession of this simple truth.

I have broken bread and wine a thousand times, but now this really was communion. A coming closer, an encounter, with God and his children. With brothers and sisters I didn't know were in the same family. Maybe in the past some of us, and our forefathers, had even preached against those of other traditions.

We had slandered other ministries, put them down, and tried to prove how our traditions and methods were superior to the churches down the road. All that was falling away, around the table of our Lord and Saviour, Jesus Christ. In his presence all our divisions were melting away.

The moment when the Spirit of unity showed me his finest work came after we'd all shared our communion perspectives. There was tangible peace in the room like a breeze that carries a fragrance. I had prayed a simple prayer of thanks for the bread and blackcurrant cordial and the elements were being passed around. Then I found myself looking up to receive the cup from a gentle lady kneeling in front of me, offering me this most precious sip. It was the Quaker. She smiled up at me and said, "Here is the blood of Christ, shed for you." Fountains opened within me, a flash flood of grace bursting through barriers of pride and arrogance in my heart. For sure the Spirit of God was on the move within me, as he had been moving among us on that retreat.

United...

When the Spirit of God moves, he unites those who seek to humbly follow.

What we tasted on that retreat is just a miniscule glimpse of a worldwide move of God. It is my deepest conviction that what we saw was a foretaste of heaven and a strong urge from God for us to "get it together". To grow together, to keep together.

This is not just relevant to inter-church fraternals or the world of ministers and leaders. Across the body of Christ there is a refreshing call to enjoy the blessing that comes from the unity of the Spirit. There is a global movement of people who are recognising the significance of gathering together, across history's divides and beyond the hardened barriers of our structures.

This story is far from over, and the best is still ahead of us. As we consider with care what we see, however dry and deserted it may appear, may we envision so much more. May we learn to drink from the never-ending well of the Holy Spirit who unites us and, as we share what we enjoy, may we see our communities transformed by this living water.

Part 1:
The Cry for a United Kingdom

If you're aware in your own heart and life of scars left by division and broken relationships, this book is for you. If you stand with me and look across the wreckage of shattered promises, fractured homes, divided churches and competing denominations, and dream of something richer, deeper, truer, this book should add fuel to that hopeful fire within.

Perhaps, like me, you've had enough of the independent empires of men that fill us with pride and drain our communities of blessing, and deep within you there is a longing for the kingdom of God to be more evident in our world? You may Google the list of multiple churches in your neighbourhood and ask, "Is all this division what Jesus intended?"

You may be earnestly leading a church forward and yet be sincerely concerned about compromising your convictions in the name of "unity". You may have nightmares of standing in circles next to people with no dress-sense singing, "Bind Us Together" in an inter-denominational hug-in and cringe at the thought. (If you're too young to know that song, ask your aunty Susan!)

But then again you get a sense it isn't a case of sitting cross-legged and glassy-eyed singing Lennon's "Imagine" either, mystically unifying the universe in a nebulous bond of humanness. You may wonder deeply about the true essence of unity and if there are any boundaries to it all, and if it's still okay to believe unity in Christ leaves some people behind. If so, who decides who's in and how do we deal with that?

Or maybe you're simply devastated by another divorce, another boardroom breakup, a team collapse or a church split and the spreading desert of division in our fragmented world. At the hard end of the issues we'll be grappling with here are broken hearts and muted dreams. Maybe yours.

Perhaps the reason for reading is less dramatic. You are leading a team and see the potential for achieving great things in your organisation, but too often that progress is halted by discord and disunity. You're a church leader and you want to see your community blessed by your ministry, but this seems hampered by internal arguments over loyalties, titles, rotas, who chooses the songs on Sunday, or how, since Socially Inept Ian was sent our way, our small group has never been the same.

Or maybe at home there is too much shouting, or too much silence, and you wonder if your spouse, even your whole family, is pulling in the same direction. Will you ever be able to get it together?

Whatever your reason for picking up this book, I invite you on a voyage of new discoveries and awakened memories. As much as any time in history, we need to rediscover the *power of one*. Our disjointed society is thirsty for the refreshing difference of a united kingdom. There are rich, powerful promises flowing from the Scriptures about the beauty of unity and the consequences for those who enjoy it. Beyond that, communities and nations are blessed with life when we, the people, live out unity in Christ.

Even further, beyond the goal of blessing others lies our ultimate destination: the glory of God in the heavens and on the earth. Unity is a picture of our glorious end. We must not give up this pursuit, nor be deceived by the devil of division who silences conversation and sows seeds of discord even while we sleep.

We'll navigate these swirling seas with the rudder of simple, but I trust strong, theology. Because I am more of a thoughtful practitioner than abstract theorist, instead of writing an essay for academic plaudits I'll be working with you to lay some theological foundations to build on for the future. Before we get to Part 2's exploration of Ephesians and the starting point of it all (God), in Part 1 we'll keep tuning in to his ancient cry for a united kingdom, recognising that we are surveying the wreckage of the wars and factions of millennia.

This is not a new challenge.

On the battlefields of homes and households we still walk, with the carnage of doctrinal divisions and church leadership battles all around us. If you listen carefully, and give full attention, the trumpet of heaven can still be heard, sounding a hope-filled call to unity in the name of Christ.

1
Fragmented:
Surveying the Wreckage

"We don't have a unitary society any more, you know; it's very fragmented. I look up and down my block in Silverlake and there is a different universe in every house."

–Janet Fitch

To set the scene it would be easy to look up some statistics to demonstrate the increasing fragmentation of Western society, quoting significant scholars and their research on the disintegration of our communities. Much has been written and said about the increasing "popularity" of single-occupancy dwellins, with more Britons than ever living in a home with no spouse, partner or other family member. We don't need statistics to show us this is not good for our society.

Think of the people in your neighbourhood, like the elderly widow that no one visits any more. Fast-paced families don't have time to stop and listen. Think about the suburban computer geek up the road from you whose strongest sense of community may well be with gaming buddies living on Yap Street, Kuala Lumpur or in a high-rise apartment block in the banking district of Lagos. They're connected; they've built homes together in *Minecraft* and fearlessly defeated the Taliban in *Call of Duty,* but in so many ways, their disconnection from social realities is haunting. It leaves them fearful of asking the girl next door out on a date.

And as for that girl, what lies ahead for her? When her father left a few months ago, the Disney vision of her own marriage to a faithful man was obliterated. Her heart's compass was spinning and the drunken mistakes she made on Friday night are now plastered by so-called friends all over the social networks. She has no friends and has lost faith in family.

You see, we only need to look around us and see the devastation of division. It is in our streets, it is in our towns and cities, sadly often precipitated by us Christians arrogantly pursuing our own agendas and failing to work with the kingdom of God as our focus. Division is still rife in our nation. Independence reigns (even while Elizabeth occupies the throne). As I write, the political momentum is towards devolution and the division of political power to nations and even regions. We could end up with the Nation of Cornwall being established within our lifetimes. Who would have thought?

I know these are sweeping generalisations, but hear me as the caring uncle saying, "You're not well" rather than the medical specialist diagnosing *acute viral rhinopharyngitis.*[1]

The point is clear: our society is sick.

We are losing the art of conversation, the art of truly listening to each other. We're burying our heads in our smartphones and social feeds and ignoring, alienating, people who we perceive are not like us. So what is God's answer? What is the role of Christians in this world? Do we see the devastation of division all around us, turn a blind eye and walk away or do we ask for greater insight into God's plan for the world he loves?

What about the Church? What kind of people do we need to become in order to bring restoration amongst the wreckage? How will this change our friendships, our families and our churches? What about the potential that deep, lasting unity in the Church will bring blessing to our towns, cities and even the nation?

This simple book sets out to explore the principle of unity and the promise of heaven's blessing – the unique power of Christian unity to rebuild a palace for the King in the wasteland of our selfish wars. Next we will go on a pilgrim's journey from a dusty desert hideaway three thousand years ago to today's global village. We'll rediscover God's joyful Master Plan to bring us together, embracing the conversations and the cost, to see his dream become reality.

Endnotes
1. Otherwise known as the common cold.

2
Dew in a Dry Land

"In the sweetness of friendship let there be laughter and sharing of pleasures. For in the dew of little things the heart finds its morning and is refreshed."

–Khalil Gibran

So where did all this division really begin? Who started us off in the wrong key? Can we learn, will we learn, from the stories of old? As we take a brief walk through long centuries of disharmony, we'll read a poem, hear a song, from one leader who seemed to get this unity thing. Don't you just love chapters that end with a poem? But first, the beginning…

Since the cataclysmic fall of Adam and Eve[2] and that first murder, of Abel by his brother Cain[3], the earth has been stained by the blood of division. Adam and Eve's "marriage" of harmony was ruptured by their rebellion against God, resulting in enmity with each other. This was passed down to their sons who started sibling rivalry off with a bloody murder. The story of humanity is scarred with selfishness and disunity, a condition that has wrought havoc and ruined lives every generation since. The opening scenes of this tragedy are played out on the dusty plains of the Ancient Near East, and I'm among the perplexed when reading the story, surprised and confused at times, given God's apparent role in it all.

In Genesis 11 we read the famous but bizarre story of the Tower of Babel. I must have read it a hundred times since Sunday School and it still furrows my brow. The Almighty seems threatened by the empire-building power of linguistic (and therefore cultural?) unity amongst Adam's sons and daughters, so he uses his power to bring division, to scatter. Great start to a book on unity!

"'Look!' he said. 'The people are united, and they all speak the same language. After this, nothing they set out to do will be impossible for them! Come, let's go down and confuse the people with different languages. Then they won't be able to understand each other.'"[4]

As an ancient tale explaining how we came to have all these languages scattered around the world it offers a primitive thesis; as a parable warning us of our instinctive desire to build towers and great cities "for ourselves"[5] it shows us that nothing is new. Greater thinkers than I will also explore what it tells us about how our Creator intervenes (or not) in human affairs according to his mysterious will. What do you make of it?

The Babel epic has been preached so often to inspire hearers to work towards unity because "nothing is impossible" for those who do, but I would suggest a different lesson. Within a greater plan, God's Master Plan, there is a truer, deeper, more vibrant unity available here that is made even more powerful because of the diversity of cultures. Maybe the Lord was not threatened, for his own sake, by mono-cultural, linguistic unity; perhaps the scattering of languages and the creation of multiple cultures is attributed to him in this story because he had something better up his sleeve?

Enter Abram, son of Terah, a nomad on the way to somewhere, sent by the Lord. God makes him a promise concerning his own (non-existent) family, and this covenant is about the blessing of nations:

"I will make you into a great nation. I will bless you and make you famous, and you will be a blessing to others. I will bless those who bless you and curse those who treat you with contempt. All the families on earth will be blessed through you."[6]

We glean from this foundational story, with its twists and turns and far-reaching implications, a simple observation: at this crucial juncture of God's rescue plan for humanity his promise is to bring blessing to all nations. Not do to away with the nations altogether, undoing Babel, or choosing his favourites and forever forgetting the rest. Rather, according to Genesis, the Master's plan is to show his faithfulness to all nations by working his purposes out in one culture, one family line, with a view of establishing on earth his kingdom of diversity, uniting people from every tribe and tongue and nation.

As we sweep through the stories of the Patriarchs on long journeys between deserts and fertile hills, we see the Abrahamic covenant tested, proven, compromised, left in tatters. The God of Abraham, Isaac and Jacob proves faithful, yet the people swerve towards division and discord at almost every turn. It's a torrid, now familiar tale. Families and tribes war against each other, fathers have favourites and we, the people, find a thousand reasons to complain. A lot. In Exodus the Lord's beloved, covenant people get fed up with his inconvenient scheduling and make gods with their own hands. In the dry Sinai desert we would hear heaven's cry for people to unite with the Lord as their King, their ruler, if it wasn't for the drunken din of the party at The Golden Calf.[7]

In all this we are just glancing at centuries of heartache and discord, tribal factions and broken promises, with the Promised Land as our backdrop. On the journey we arrive with God's covenant people, Israel, to a land of milk and honey. And big grapes. And big, big giants. The Exodus is behind us and we now have the presence of God manifest in the Ark of the Covenant, settling in a land of our own. Or is it a land that was our own, and we just came back? In fact, it is a land which many others consider their own. Oh dear, this is going to be messy. For millennia, it's still messy. Whose land is it, anyway?[8]

My point is this, by the time we get to David's kingdom (and I promise we'll get to the poem bit soon) there have been generations and tribes, families and factions fighting over a small (but fertile) piece of land in the Middle East. During the period of Judges there had been countless wars, prophecies and sorceries, failed leaders and times when it seemed that God had given up on Israel altogether.

But in fact it was the other way round: in the ultimate act of rejection, the people beg the Lord (their eternal King) for a king of their own, like the other nations.[9] The prophet Samuel delivers the message and feels God's pain. So you want a king of your own? What kind of kingdom are you seeking? The answer is found in the tragic tale of Saul, Israel's first king, sliding from merciful anointing into murderous insanity. It gets worse before it gets better. Read it and you'll weep.

However (and praise God for his glorious howevers), by his infinite grace, and in keeping with his promise, the Lord finds a man he can trust. A king whose throne he will establish forever – David.

You may have heard or read that David's life was not free from bloodshed or adultery, and for sure too many authors and preachers gloss over the details of his life to make him out as "a hero who slipped up once" when the story is more human, more frail, than we dare admit. Be that as it may, the quality that led the Lord to anoint him was his heart.[10] It resonated with the rhythm of heaven, the eternal kingdom.

As Gene Edwards portrays so powerfully in his classic book, *The Tale of Three Kings*, David was a king of a different order. He was hunted down by a jealous King Saul and dodged the spears without throwing them back.[11] Later in life, his family divided and Absalom his successor rebelled against him, dividing the people. David's broken heart was still after God's: he wouldn't pick up a spear to throw in judgment on his rebel son. As Edwards tells the story, Abishai his friend commends David's refusal to divide the kingdom:

> *"Saul was evil toward you and made your life torture. You responded only with respect and private agony... You fled rather than cause division. You risked your life for unity and sealed your lips and eyes to all injustices."*[12]

That's a beautiful insight and it sets the scene for David's heavenly poetry in Psalm 133. By the time this poem, this song of ascending steps is written, so much has taken place to bring David to a deep conviction about The Power of One. He fled from Saul to the cave of Adullam and emerges into the light as the leader of a ragtag bunch of misfits and outlaws. Into that cave arrived 400 individuals, including family members and criminals on the run. With David as their captain they learned to stick together.[13] At other times, David forged loyalties with a faithful band of warriors, his mighty men willing to kill for the sake of blessing him with fresh water.[14] From their togetherness as a band of brothers, victories and folklore followed. David was a man who had tasted unity and, under his reign, God's people had enjoyed its fruit.

Furthermore, as an introduction to his psalm, we must recognise David's desire and heart for the presence of God. It is explicit in his writings and evident in his biographies. He danced half-naked without shame before the Ark of the Covenant, so thrilled to see God's presence take centre stage in David's city.[15] He was a king of passionate worship, submitted in love and humility to the eternal King of heaven. It seems he longed for the presence of God more than anything else. Though he was anointed as king of a great empire, his heart longed for the eternal kingdom spoken of by the prophet. His heart rejoiced to see people gather in Jerusalem, the holy city fed by the spring of Gihon at the foot of his palace. It seems he was not just thrilled to see them gather under his king-ship for a drink, but he rejoiced to see hearts even more deeply refreshed by the eternal fountain of God's presence. I reckon all of this is in the mix when he writes this psalm. Perhaps he is later on in life and recalling his anointing at Hebron, that day the Ark returned to Jerusalem, or maybe other things he's seen and heard, taught and tasted. I imagine him reflecting on the evils he has seen, even those he has committed, and savouring the sweetest things he has experienced in his life, so he turns to write… about unity. The refreshing, supernatural unity of the Spirit of God:

"How good and pleasant it is when God's people live together in unity! It is like precious oil poured on the head, running down on the beard, running down on Aaron's beard, down on the collar of

his robe. It is as if the dew of Hermon were falling on Mount Zion. For there the Lord bestows his blessing, even life for evermore."[16]

What a beautiful poem. An inspiring song of unity, set against a background of generations of discord.

It is indeed good, pleasant (the Hebrew word can also mean "sweetly sounding") when God's people live, dwell together in unity. The word *yachad* in Hebrew is sometimes translated "harmony" and this an idea we will come back to. David the musician is reflecting here on the sweet-sounding harmony of people coming together, with one vision, one purpose, to one place, with a view to dwelling together.

As we have read, he describes it as the abundant, overflowing anointing oil on Aaron the priest. David would have been told stories as a boy of this moment in Israel's history, where the priest was set apart, cleansed, consecrated, made holy under heaven's gaze and by heaven's order.[17] Unity is like that oil, dripping all over the body of the priest. Harmony sets apart God's people, whatever their background or failings, cleansing, removing the odour of the journey, preparing them to offer acceptable worship. There is even a suggestion here that unity defines God's people set apart amongst the nations, kissed with anointing from heaven. Has David the priest-king tasted of the future "kingdom of priests" of which we now, in Christ belong?

What is clear is that David is inspired with a vision of the impossible made possible, of the far-reaching consequences of genuine unity in God's kingdom. I have been privileged to sit on Mount Zion and hold my hand in Gihon's spring on a sunny day, imagining how dry, how thirsty, that land was before irrigation systems and desalination plants. Even a cursory look at Jerusalem's archaeology and geology will illustrate just how important that spring was. It was a dry mountain region and permanent settlements surrounded water sources. Their lives depended on it. The Gihon was worth fighting over (ask David[18]) and was walled in, defended at great cost. You get the picture; in David's time Jerusalem was typically dry and most of the year water was in scarce supply, from a single source.

In contrast, this psalm mentions another mountain 190 kilometres away in the north of David's kingdom, namely Mount Hermon. At this higher latitude and altitude, the mountain tops are almost covered year-round with snow. For sure, the air is cool and the dew is refreshing, dependable, pure, as if from heaven. The result on Hermon's foothills? Lush groves and rich grass, thriving forests and life. Colour, fresh air, fruit.

Ah, unity. God's love shared between God's people. It's as if the dew of Hermon, so clean and pure, so widespread and life-giving, is falling on Jerusalem's dry, sun-baked hill.

This is David's song, his life-lesson. In a fractured world of warfare and short-lived kingdoms a dynamic is at work, a challenging pursuit, an ideal of heaven's origin: unity. In God's house; under his instruction. Here is the blessing of life, even life everlasting. You see, in that place where there is this unity, God bestows, commands, gives out a blessing. On the place, through the people, from heaven's throne, the King of kings speaks out a blessing. I hope your heart is stirred and your taste-buds whetted; we have much to explore. There is great power in oneness and for the sake of where we live, where we work and worship, our lives must stay in tune with this refreshing, life-giving song.

The cry of heaven was heard by David and echoes through his writings and those of the prophets after him who lamented over the divided kingdoms. God's heart is for unity in the nations; for a united kingdom. So what does this look like and didn't Jesus the eternal king, the son of David, fix all this? That will be our next port of call...

Endnotes:

2. Genesis 3
3. Genesis 4:1-12
4. Genesis 11:7
5. Genesis 11:4
6. Genesis 12:2-3
7. Exodus 32:1-29
8. No answers found here.
9. 1 Samuel 8:1-9
10. 1 Samuel 13:13-14 – Because Saul was disobedient to the Lord, even while the throne was still occupied by King Saul, the Lord 'sought out' a man who was worthy of establishing a forever kingdom. David was that man, as confirmed via the prophet in 1 Samuel 16:12
11. Edwards, 1992, 36
12. Ibid., 71
13. 1 Samuel 22:1-2
14. For an inspiring list of exploits and mighty followers of King David, see 2 Samuel 23:8ff
15. 2 Samuel 6:16
16. Psalm 133 (NIV)
17. See Leviticus 8 and Exodus 29
18. 2 Samuel 5

3
The Prayer Still Unanswered

"I pray that they will all be one"
– Jesus of Nazareth

I first became a follower of Christ when I was just 4 years old.
I vaguely recall a day when, in a home group kids' Bible class, I
prayed a prayer. I decided I didn't want to go to hell. My parents
were thrilled and I genuinely believe heaven smiled too. Between
then and now there have been other life-changing moments
where my relationship with Jesus went up several gears in just one
moment. For instance, when I was publicly baptised to declare
my faith to others (with a swimming party at Hewett School in
Norwich afterwards). Even more vivid than that, I will never
forget the first time I felt the in-filling of the Holy Spirit (I felt like
a fire had started in the core of my stomach), the powerful light-
filled dream I had when I woke up in the middle of the night,
sweating, having encountered God in such an undeniable way.

Subsequently, I am grateful to have seen a few significant
healing miracles take place before my own eyes and there have

been monumental moments of answered prayer in the last twenty years of marriage, most significantly the end of my wife Helen's (thankfully brief) brush with terminal cancer and the breaking off of chains of barrenness. We cried out in Jesus' name and the King of heaven answered. Three wonderful children later, I have absolute confidence in God's ability to answer prayer.

But my heart aches for all the prayers unanswered. There are those prayers that only God could have answered, like when our colleague Jenny's life ebbed away in Watford General Hospital despite our pleas round her bed that the Lord would extend her tenure with those she served so well. Heaven was silent. One word from HQ and she'd still be with us today. Silence. More significantly, and this is where we are going in this chapter, there are those prayers we pray that are unanswered because they require the cooperation of others.

Helen and I have been leading Wellspring Church now for the best part of 17 years and somewhere in heaven's inbox there are a thousand prayers we've prayed that have yet to receive a reply. These are the prayers that needed someone to change their minds; someone to save their own marriage, to let go of their own unforgiveness; to share their own faith in their own workplace. Ah, the pain of leadership! We can do our utmost to teach, and show, and demonstrate, and exhort, and even pray, with a view to people changing their ways, and the bud fails to flower. Despite our best efforts and our deepest pleadings, the branch doesn't yield any fruit. You don't even have to be a church leader to feel this pain in fact; we all know the agony of unanswered prayer.

So does Jesus.

In Philip Yancey's excellent book, *Prayer: Does it Make Any Difference?* we marvel with him (and so many other writers on spirituality) at this strangely comforting reality: not all of Jesus's prayers were answered either. On the cross he cried out to the one who could save him from death, but he was not saved from the most painful death imaginable.[19] Jesus was acquainted with the sorrow of unanswered prayer and one particular prayer remains unanswered. Even still.

As we continue this heavenward exploration, taking his rightful place at the helm of our ship is, of course, Captain Jesus, son of David. With hundreds of years of discord, division and disharmony in Israel since David sang Psalm 133 in Jerusalem, Jesus is sent to the villages and hamlets of Galilee in search of Abraham's sons and daughters. His goal? To unite them in the establishment of a new kingdom, his own band of "mighty men" (and women) who would be the first of a new, priestly kingdom. What a mission: amongst the working-class fishing communities, the rural outposts, the unschooled and uncouth, Jesus was to call a tiny group of disciples to follow him and change history forever.

Many would have started this pursuit somewhere else, chosen from the cream of the crop rather than from the fringes of the fields, but not Jesus. He would live for them and love them without condition; he would heal some of their bodies and bring hope to all their hearts; his teaching would confuse and confound them and fill them with wonder of a kingdom unlike the Roman rule that oppressed them, or the Herods that had tormented them. For three years Jesus would do all he could to show them the ways of this new kingdom and then on The Weekend That Changed It All, he would die, and rise again to deal a humiliating, fatal blow to the enemy. Satan, the devil of destruction and division, was sent reeling from Jesus' victory and the raging battle for men and women's hearts and minds remains in its final throes.

Even still, as so many have lamented in prayers, poetry and countless books and articles, the plea of the Christus Victor remains answered. This was a prayer for unity. For the followers of Jesus to be reunited; and we are God's answer.

We should remember that Jesus had visited Jerusalem often as a child and, in the three years of his recorded "ministry" as the disciples' leader, he went to the Temple courts to teach. I wonder if each time he came across the effluent of Roman rule with its disregard for dignity and suppression of commoners, he sensed new levels of the Father's pain for the people of that city? This city that had stoned the prophets, silencing (for a time) their warnings, was now ruled by a Temple system corrupt and compromised. Jerusalem was a city scarred by centuries of war and disharmony, and the so-called "rule" of Israel's kings and tribal leaders had become a sad story of failure and idolatry. Almost forgotten were the great days of the City of David and the simple heartfelt pageantry of a city centred on the worship of the Almighty. Empires of men had all but replaced the kingdom of heaven. By the time Jesus walked the rugged streets of Jerusalem, his message to the people of God, to the residents and travelling pilgrims, was an ancient call to repent, to turn back.

That sense comes across in Luke's gospel as he recalls in pain Jesus' heartfelt desire:

"O Jerusalem, Jerusalem, the city that kills the prophets and stones God's messengers! How often I have wanted to gather your children together as a hen protects her chicks beneath her wings, but you wouldn't let me. And now, look, your house is abandoned. And you will never see me again until you say, 'Blessings on the one who comes in the name of the Lord!'"[20]

Foretelling his future entry on a donkey into the city as the

Son of David, the Saviour King who would fulfil Psalm 118, Jesus expresses the heart of God to bring people together, to unite Jerusalem's children into the house of the Lord.

Within months, perhaps even weeks of this heartfelt outburst overlooking the holy city, Jesus is back in the city during Passover, surrounded by pilgrims and looking a lonely death in the face. He is crying out to the Father, praying that unanswered prayer.

John the evangelist crafts his gospel so powerfully. Before we read Jesus' unanswered prayer in John 17 we must see the context: in Chapter 13 we're in the upper room amazed by the washing of the disciples' feet (and admonishment to follow Jesus' example[21]), a disturbing prediction of his betrayal by Judas Iscariot[22] and the foretelling of outright denial by Simon Peter.[23] Gut-wrenching stuff. Jesus comforts and teaches in John 14, reiterating his own identity as the Son sent by the Father (a running theme in this gospel), bringing the glory of heaven to earth. Then we hear Jesus promising the Advocate, the Holy Spirit, a gift to be sent "to lead into all truth"[24] and as the "ruler of this world approaches"[25] (to lead him to a painful death and great sadness) Jesus urges his followers to love one another, remaining in him, the true Vine.[26] It is hard not to be deeply moved as we read through this section of John's gospel. The richness of these teachings has inspired and intrigued millions of words – those of scholars and Sunday School teachers, preachers and mystics.

"Then his disciples said, 'At last you are speaking plainly and not figuratively. Now we understand that you know everything, and there's no need to question you. From this we believe that you came from God.' Jesus asked, 'Do you finally believe? But the time is coming—indeed it's here now—when you will be scattered, each one going his own way, leaving me alone. Yet I

am not alone because the Father is with me. I have told you all this so that you may have peace in me. Here on earth you will have many trials and sorrows. But take heart, because I have overcome the world.'"[27]

Join me as we sit there, our mouths wide open at our Rabbi's last teaching, before we head for the Garden of his betrayal, before we hear Jesus pray. His prediction lands like a bitter medicine in our hearts. We're going to be scattered, this new kingdom will (for an era) bring division, and we're even going to deny Christ when he needs us the most. We're going to have trials and sorrows. We'll have to find peace in him while on battlefields without him. We'll have to remember this promise and take heart from Jesus' reassurance.

"After saying these things, Jesus looked up to heaven and said…"[28] Then the Saviour prays. We could spend a long time drilling into every line of this intercession and many authors have written so much already. At the risk of adding yet more (repeated) comments to a familiar passage, for the sake of our journey we must find ourselves looking up to heaven alongside our Saviour and saying "amen" to this prayer. Because he is praying for us. We must say "amen" not just with our lips, but with our lives:

"I am praying not only for these disciples but also for all who will ever believe in me through their message. I pray that they will all be one, just as you and I are one—as you are in me, Father, and I am in you. And may they be in us so that the world will believe you sent me."[29]

We can clearly see this prayer is for those who have remained in him, for those who believe he is the Sent One.[30] He is not praying for "the world"[31] but rather, for those in the world he calls his own. His prayer is for oneness. The basis of this oneness is his own relationship with the Father. Within the Godhead, the holy mysterious Trinity, is the essence of the harmony Jesus prays for. Our heads explode in awe of even the concept and our hearts well up with wonder. Jesus wouldn't pray a prayer that was out of line with the will of heaven, he wouldn't ask for something the Father wasn't saying, doing, or working towards,[32] so this is a prayer that will be answered, in time… and we are the subject of that prayer. Astounding.

"I have given them the glory you gave me, so they may be one as we are one. I am in them and you are in me. May they experience such perfect unity that the world will know that you sent me and that you love them as much as you love me. Father, I want these whom you have given me to be with me where I am. Then they can see all the glory you gave me because you loved me even before the world began!"[33]

Here, in these verses, the ancient cry for a united kingdom reaches its crescendo. Even clearer than David's song for the dew of heaven to fall on God's dry hill, we hear the Son plead with his heavenly Father in that same city, for heaven's harmony to be expressed amongst his people; for a kingdom of unity and not discord. This "perfect unity" is an experience to be enjoyed and sustained, as a glorious expression of the oneness of God himself. Diverse yet unified, vibrant yet harmonised, a new community that shows this broken world his glory. Held together by the ultimate force in the world, God's selfless, perfect love, Jesus prays for us to live by his power, the unifying power of one.

If this prayer had been answered already, for sure our world would be a different place. I won't be the last author to reflect on this subject and lament, despising my own pride whilst still feeling wounded by the arrogance of others.

Come on, dear friend, let's not just kneel and lament on all that is lost. Let's lift our heads up to heaven and be the "amen" to Jesus' prayer. When our lives echo this prayer's intent, our homes can be places of glory and peace. Marriages can be strong, families can stick together. This is the power of one! When our neighbourhoods see a people united in loving unity, dignity and honour, they will catch glimpses of God's glory. Your church can be united and when it is the blessing will flow.

What's more, I am deeply convicted that the places where we live need to see the whole body of Christ, as expressed in different congregations and fellowships, uniting in prayer and praise of a common King, proclaiming the truth of another kingdom. This book has been written to encourage you, whoever you are, to embrace with greater passion a "kingdom mentality" where you live, work and worship.

We can see then that Jesus' prayer resonates with promises from heaven over the ages, the promise that a people would be blessed by God, with his glorious presence, uniting diverse nations as an expression of God's own loving nature. The Father's heart is to bring to himself, in the fullness of time, a people united in the name of his Son. All his children. As we'll explore in coming chapters, this is not a mono-cultural blandness, a mediocre ecumenism of compromised convictions. It is a vibrant, living dynamic.

It is the power of *one*.

What can we learn and what must we do to work with God in pursuit of his heart's cry, for a united kingdom of justice and dignity? We should ask what it looks like and take a good look at its foundations. So many generations have built over the rubble of the era before. We need to excavate the "Unity of the Spirit", push aside what it isn't and build afresh on what it is. In the next section we will pick up the teaching of the Apostle Paul and gain fresh perspectives on God's Master Plan.

Endnotes
19. Yancey, P, Prayer: Does It Make Any Difference, 2006, 68
20. Luke 13:34-35
21. John 13:1-17
22. John 13:1-30
23. John 13:1-38
24. John 14:17
25. John 14:30
26. John 15:1-16
27. John 16:29-33
28. John 17:1
29. John 17:20-21
30. Lloyd-Jones, 2003, 8. I find it hard to embrace with equal conviction Martyn Lloyd-Jones's own acuity about some aspects of who is 'in' and out of Christian unity in the context of John 17, his case is clear and compelling. Jesus has in mind the called-out ones, believers who have been given to Jesus by the Father.
31. John 17:9
32. John 5:19-20
33. John 17:22-24

Part 2:
Unity Starts Here

"One of the main tasks of theology is to find words that do not divide but unite, that do not create conflict but unity, that do not hurt but heal."

–Henri Nouwen

A number of years ago I found myself deeply wearied in ministry, knocked back (again) by picking up some of the shattered dreams and expectations (my own included) lying in the aftermath of a respected church leader's moral failure. Devastation of this nature has always demoralised and on this occasion I found myself strangely discouraged enough to give up on an unrelated area of ministry.

You see, I had been co-leading a unity movement called Christians Across Watford (CAW) for a number of years, something I will explain and unpack later in this book. For more than a decade we had been praying, planning, exploring and learning what it is to be "one Church in this town and for this town" and like a blindside tackle during this season of profound pastoral disappointment, my heart for Christian unity began to fail. My enthusiasm for working with other church leaders began to wane and pessimism about the place and purpose of CAW was creeping in. I was in danger of giving in, retreating, and laying down the mantle of leadership. I had lost heart for working with other churches; the colour of a once-vivid vision was fading fast. Reading Ephesians in that season was like a defibrillator for my spirit.

It was during a tearful, prayerful retreat that I picked up Paul's circular letter to the first century churches in Asia Minor (the book of Ephesians)[34] and my despairing slide was arrested. I woke up again to the centrality, the necessity, of unity in Christ. Today's Church must heed these timeless words, stepping into a greater enjoyment of the unity of the Spirit. Yes, an enjoyment! God the Father wants to get his kids together. Unity is a glorious end in itself. The King of heaven longs for us to revel in the blessing of unity in his household, and as we lay our lives, our homes, our churches, businesses and towns on this foundation, the kingdom of heaven is built, a dwelling place for his presence on the earth.

This section looks to explore God's "Master Plan" as passionately explained and pursued by the Apostle Paul. We can't hear King David's song of the beauty of unity echo round Jerusalem, nor kneel beside Jesus in that same city as he cries out for his followers to live as one, without being stirred deep within. Heaven's cry resonates with something in us that knows something needs to change, and in fact new efforts need to be made to hold onto one another in this fragmented, fractured world.

Let's not rush ahead to fix it, though. It would be reckless to build a large house without a good talk with an architect first – foundations and structure matters. Before we go much further, we need to take a step back and ask some good questions about the nature of the "Unity of the Spirit". What is it? What does it look like and how do we recognise the real thing?

Drawing centrally on Paul's letter to the Ephesian church, with references elsewhere from his writings, what is the basis of Christian unity and how can we keep it healthy in our day? This section is based on three verses in chapter 4 of Ephesians (we'll get to the rest soon enough). Here Paul explains the starting point, the reason, and the basis of our unity. We must keep this unity because:

> *"...there is one body and one Spirit, just as you have been called to one glorious hope for the future. There is one Lord, one faith, one baptism, one God and Father of all, who is over all, in all, and living through all."*[35]

Former Archbishop Rowan Williams puts it like this:

> *"Unity is first and foremost being in Christ through the Spirit. It is the unity of the very life of God; the unity in relationship of Father, Son and Spirit."*[36]

Because God has revealed himself as unified, complete, in communion with himself and enjoying perfect harmony as Father, Son and Spirit, we his people are called to enjoy the same loving unity within our communities. Why stick together? Because we have one Father, one Lord and one Spirit. Unified diversity is the very nature of God.[37] This is the power of *one*.

Endnotes

34. For insightful and detailed discussion about authorship, I recommend a read of the commentaries listed in the bibliography. For the purpose of my writing and given the nature of this book, I will write on the basis that Pauline authorship does indeed have a sound scholarly basis, as preferred by F.F. Bruce, A. M. Hunter and Findlay (see Stott, John R W, The Message of Ephesians, 1991, 21). In this good company I also recognise the validity of the thesis that Paul

writes with a broad audience of Christian churches in mind, rather than one specific group of believers.

35. Ephesians 4:4-6

36. Williams, R as cited in Slipper, C, *5 Steps to Living in Christian Unity*, 2013, 40

37. There is not room here for a thorough discussion of Trinitarian doctrine. However, the Eastern Church Fathers' understanding of *perichoresis* is worth looking up. The ideas of Athanasius and others explore how the distinct Persons of the Godhead are inextricably linked, mutually penetrating and indwelling each other whilst maintaining their unity.

4
One Father

We start our study of Ephesians with our birthright, our adoption: *"[There is] one God and Father of all, who is over all, in all, and living through all."*[38]

It is a principle central to Paul's argument throughout this epistle, a compelling and encouraging truth that speaks to a multi-ethnic first century church, where racial and religious histories threatened the fellowship's future. Though they are born of different parents, in different places, they are now (in Christ) family. In the first two chapters of Ephesians, readers are inspired to remember that they are now related, Jew and Gentile, adopted into the same household:

"All praise to God, the Father of our Lord Jesus Christ, who has blessed us with every spiritual blessing in the heavenly realms because we are united with Christ. Even before he made the world, God loved us and chose us in Christ to be holy and without fault in his eyes. God decided in advance to adopt us into his own family by bringing us to himself through Jesus Christ. This is what he wanted to do, and it gave him great pleasure."[39]

What a delightful, compelling reality. We have one Father, who for his own great pleasure decided before we even had a say, to adopt us into his own family through the sending of his Son. The first hearers of this teaching may well have looked around the bare-plastered room, lit by oil lamps, those makeshift churches in shop-fronts and side streets, at the most profoundly diverse group of new believers and wondered: "How did I end up with this bunch?" (In fact, you probably think that every Sunday, or in your house group on a mundane Wednesday evening). Paul's words inspire and answer: we are here because we're family. Because it pleased the God who made us and saved us, to adopt us into his new household.

A fundamental conviction this teaching carries, and it should undergird all our considerations henceforth, is that unity under God is already established. We are family. Adopted. Done deal. It was my friend Rev Ewen Huffman who first alerted me to this now obvious reality.[40] We do not make unity, any more than an infant orphan chooses who will adopt them. A higher power, with greater judgment than our own, a heavenly Father, chose us from among the peoples and the nations and called us his own.

"[Our Father] is so rich in kindness and grace that he purchased our freedom with the blood of his Son and forgave our sins. He has showered his kindness on us, along with all wisdom and understanding."[41]

The glorious Church, the fruit of God's Master Plan. We are his "masterpiece"[42] drawn now from almost (but not yet) all the peoples of the earth; a family, united by one Father. This unity, this inheritance, was paid for at great cost, and is precious beyond our comprehension.

Paul puts it plainly to the "newbies" in the family:

"Don't forget that you Gentiles used to be outsiders. You were called 'uncircumcised heathens' by the Jews, who were proud of their circumcision, even though it affected only their bodies and not their hearts. In those days you were living apart from Christ. You were excluded from citizenship among the people of Israel, and you did not know the covenant promises God had made to them. You lived in this world without God and without hope."[43]

But now these people who were orphans have been "brought near" to the Father.[44] As Paul goes on to explain:

"So now you Gentiles are no longer strangers and foreigners. You are citizens along with all of God's holy people. You are members of God's family."[45]

This teaching could not be more profound and I hope you will glimpse some of the wonder that must have filled the hearts of those first hearers. Imagine the scene: Jacob the faithful Jew, a trader working away from home in Ephesus had heard about the Messiah from Nazareth and when he saw the apostles performing miracles in Jesus' name, he believed. Jacob's baptism was a joyful day; his whole family joined him in public confession of their faith in Jesus the Christ. The Holy Spirit had filled him with joy and now he made it to the fellowship meetings whenever his work allowed.

Sitting opposite Jacob around the table of fellowship that day is a divorced widow, Adelpha. Her husband died at a young age fighting with the Roman legion and her only means of earning a living since has been in the pagan temple, as a prostitute. Her heart had been broken, her spirit tormented, her dignity lost. She became a follower of Christ through the witness of a friend, and since her own baptism eternal hope had flooded her soul. She had come home.

Now the letter arrives from Paul, hand delivered to be read by an elder after the Lord's Supper had been eaten and prayers of thanks had been offered. Jacob looks across the room at Adelpha while this passage is read. He hears, "You are family. She is your sister. She was an outsider, a foreigner. Before Christ, you would never have eaten a meal together. Now you do, because she is family." With the smile of God's Spirit, Adelpha looks Jacob in the eye, with love for her brother and her sisters sitting near, and because of the blood of Christ, all are equal in God's sight. They have one Father, forever.

I hope you haven't glazed over reading this, lost in a moment from the front of a Hallmark card, a Norman Rockwell painting or airbrushed cover of OK magazine. This is no glossy moment of make-believe, it is a profound, stirring reality that applies to all who believe. The essential truth for all peoples, regardless of background or culture, race or heritage, is that the work of Christ is complete. We are family, now, already. We don't make unity, it has already been gloriously, eternally achieved.[46]

We will move further on in our wonder, and perhaps next time we look across a Christian meeting, a church service, a home group, we might well smile at God's sense of humour. The joy and the pain of being family, of course, is that we don't get to choose who is in and who is out! Surrounded in your church by people not like you? Most likely you will be and bizarrely that's how God intends to bring hope and glory to this earth.

Let's move on in our quest, with fresh commitment to be about the Father's business…

Endnotes
38. Ephesians 4:6
39. Ephesians 4:3-5

40. His MA dissertation (May 2009) explores the prospects of building a missional city in Winchester through inter-church cooperation.
41. Ephesians 1:7
42. Ephesians 2:10
43. Ephesians 3:11f
44. Ephesians 3:13
45. Ephesians 3:19
46. See Lloyd-Jones' comments on John 17: 2003, 11

5
One Lord

Surveying the foundations of our unity, we return to the reasons
Paul gives for us to make every effort to stick together:

"There is one Lord, one faith, one baptism..."[47]

The apostle points out the obvious, so I am going to follow suit.
Sometimes the obvious things are overlooked. We have one Lord,
Jesus Christ, who alone has saved us (whoever we are) and whose
resurrection life is shared with us.

It is pivotal and fundamental to our unity:

*"God has now revealed to us his mysterious plan regarding
Christ, a plan to fulfil his own good pleasure. And this is the
plan: At the right time he will bring everything together under
the authority of Christ—everything in heaven and on earth.
Furthermore, because we are united with Christ, we have
received an inheritance from God, for he chose us in advance,
and he makes everything work out according to his plan."*[48]

God's Master Plan? To joyfully, with great pleasure, unite
everything under the lordship of Christ. This is not a weak plan
with vague parameters. As Lloyd-Jones provocatively states,

"The teaching of the New Testament is quite clear… there is an absolute foundation, an irreducible minimum, without which the term 'Christian' is meaningless…"

He goes on to explain that this is, "the doctrine concerning Jesus Christ, and him crucified, and justification by faith only… apart from that there is no such thing as fellowship, no basis of unity at all."[49]

We may wince at the starkness of this statement, but we should do so with one ear turned to the provocative, controversial proclamations of Jesus himself. Here we dip our toes in hot water, as we cannot ignore the divisive nature of Jesus' ministry. Mention must be given to this, lest our exploration of this subject become bland and one-dimensional. By some accounts, Jesus was a divider. Consider Jesus' words as he approached the cross:

"I have a terrible baptism of suffering ahead of me, and I am under a heavy burden until it is accomplished. Do you think I have come to bring peace to the earth? No, I have come to divide people against each other! From now on families will be split apart, three in favour of me, and two against—or two in favour and three against."[50]

Jesus is giving his followers a profound warning: don't think even for a moment that following me will get easier. This teaching and observation is unashamedly displayed in all the gospels. John's account of Jesus' life repeatedly comments on the crowds' response to Jesus' claims about himself, stating that opinions were divided about him.[51] In his life and ministry, Jesus did as much to divide communities as unite them. What do we do with this? How do we respond to that? It gives great comfort to any who have tried to share with unbelievers about our faith, seeking to introduce them to Jesus. Many people actually met Jesus in the flesh, saw the signs, ate his miraculous bread, and heard the wisdom of heaven with the ultimate anointing, and they walked away. In true humility, Jesus let them and gave his twelve closest disciples the option to do the same.[52] Jesus has always divided opinion and never forces his followers.

As we consider further what it means to be united with one Lord, we cannot escape what we have read and seen of Jesus: unity in his name will leave some people behind. Those who refuse to acknowledge his name cannot be united with him any more than someone who refuses to come into your house can share Sunday lunch with your family.[53] What I share here is my own conviction, namely that we are wiser to plead ignorance to some of the things we don't fully understand whilst saying what we see when we read the gospels. I see a Jesus who calls people to follow him, fully accepting that not everyone will. Though rejection pains him, and ultimately killed him, he did not (and does not) protest against it.

We return to Ephesians now, aware that we are called to be united in one common faith, faith in Jesus. Fifty seven times in the epistle Paul refers to "Jesus" or "Christ" as he paints a picture of God's glorious Church, living in harmony, strong in spiritual battle and empowered by the Holy Spirit, under the lordship, the authority of his God's son. What's more (and as we have just read), we are not just united with one another under Christ, but we are mysteriously united with Christ, made alive with him. Isn't this what we celebrate in the rite of baptism? In Christian baptism, in the name of Father, Son and Holy Spirit, we celebrate not just the cleansing of our sin. That is part of it, but since antiquity the people of God have engaged in ritual cleansing to prepare them for acceptable worship. All over Galilee and Judaea there were thousands of cleansing baths in the time of Jesus. Yet there was something new in the baptism of Jesus and that is the celebration of new life in Christ. Resurrection life! Paul explains,

"For he raised us from the dead along with Christ and seated us with him in the heavenly realms because we are united with Christ Jesus."[54]

This is the basis of our fellowship: we have one Lord, the same Lord, who has resurrected us (to save us from our sin and selfishness) and united us through his sacrifice to share with him the power and glory of his kingdom. Brevity precludes a fuller exploration of this here, but it is essential for us to recognise and celebrate these truths, for they form the foundation of our unity.

We are united not in belief, not in abstraction and not in culture. We are united in Christ our Lord. It is God's finest work, his masterpiece, that the likes of you and me, and billions before us, are brought together to display God's glory and bring heaven to earth in Jesus' name. Paul writes with such exuberance about letting us see the blueprint of the Architect's greatest work:

"I was chosen to explain to everyone this mysterious plan that God, the Creator of all things, had kept secret from the beginning. God's purpose in all this was to use the church to display his wisdom in its rich variety to all the unseen rulers and authorities in the heavenly places. This was his eternal plan, which he carried out through Christ Jesus our Lord. Because of Christ and our faith in him, we can now come boldly and confidently into God's presence..."[55]

If you consider Christ your Lord, your ruler, your leader, recognise again today you are not alone. Your faith was never, will never be, simply your faith. Our faith is shared and that faith is in the risen Christ who has united us with him, and in him, and he is putting us on display for all the powers of earth and heaven to see his work.

I remember standing as Chaplain to the Watford branch of John Lewis department store, admiring huge room-size rugs worth thousands of pounds, admiring the intricacy, accuracy and vibrancy of the patterns. I figured if someone could afford £9,000 for one rug, they must be able to afford a room big enough to fit it in! The friendly shop assistant, a young Muslim man who I often stopped to chat with over the years, offering to pray for him and his family, asked me if I wanted to see the back of these rugs. So I did and I was amazed to see the morass of mashed-up thread and chaotic patterns on the reverse of these beautiful, unique works of art. The pattern was almost unrecognisable. Even though the backs of the rugs had been sealed, you could still see what a confusing mess of thread-ends and knots lay on their other side. Hand-tied in Persia, for hundreds of hours by skilful artists with disciplined fingers, these masterpieces are impressive on one side and yet a bit of a mess on the other.

I use this analogy to reflect on what Paul has just taught us: God's greatest work, the result of his Master Plan, is to put on display a glorious, vibrant Church. He is making a spectacle of us by uniting us in Christ, uniting us with Christ, and in doing so revealing the richness of his wisdom in all its infinite variety and beauty, to powers unseen. The trouble is, I guess, that we typically see the ragged edges on the back of the rug. We look and wonder if this is the work of a child, and we doubt the integrity of the designer. Too often we look at the Church, or our local expression of God's people, and all we see is the tatty loose ends and mixed up patterns. We live in that agonising but creative tension between the finished work of Christ on the cross and the "work in progress" of his glorious Church. We're not all we will be, for sure, and we are challenged to make every effort to cooperate with the Lord's uniting work. Paul gives us a glimpse of the other side of the rug. Only a glimpse for now, of God's greatest work, but for sure it is enough to spur us on until the day we long for, when the finished work will be all the world can see. More of that later.

Meanwhile, back to our foundations: we are united by one faith in one Lord, who has shared with us in baptism his resurrection power. This is ultimately the only hope for a fragmented, fractured world and forms the inclusive, transformational basis of a new community that brings heaven to earth. I love how this is depicted in the book of Acts. In Luke's honest, inspiring retelling of the early Church's adventure from the Upper Room to the "ends of the earth", there is one phrase, one thing that becomes the trademark of the believers. Before they are called "Christians"[56] they are known as people who call on, live by, profess, and draw their identity from, "the Name".[57] They were people of The Name, the name of Jesus. Without Jesus they had no faith, no identity, no reason to meet and no purpose to pursue.

So it should be with us, today.

We are united in Christ, by Christ, for Christ. Isn't this the essence of the Lord's Supper? It is his meal. We gather around his table with his death, his sacrifice, at the centre. We'll come back to this table later in the book as it has enormous significance for our unity. Who we eat with and why we eat with them, defines us. I have been reflecting a lot on the dangers of diluting the power of table fellowship when we meet each other in Jesus' name. We have too often (in Charismatic/Pentecostal churches I've grown up in, anyway) moved communion to the periphery of our gatherings. I am deeply convicted about this. This simple meal, which I have shared with the elders in a village in South Sudan (it was a Ritz cracker and warm Coke) as well as ten thousand young people in a tent in Somerset (at Soul Survivor), is the message of our faith in a meal. It is encountering God, powerfully, intimately, supernaturally, with Jesus taking centre stage. It is the most glorious gift to help us remember him, because here we are careful to recite his words, remember his sacrifice and proclaim his death until he comes.[58] As Paul explains: *"though we are many, we all eat from one loaf of bread, showing that we are one body."*[59] We are one body, gathering around a common table, celebrating our unity in Christ.

Though this book is a call to unity, the last thing I would want my thoughts and questions to do is take our eyes off the Saviour. As we have already established, harmony in God's household is based on the finished work of Christ uniting us with him. It is not something we can create; it is a dynamic we are urged to maintain and expected to enjoy. If we can wonder what image is being formed on the "good" side of this rug called the Church, surely it is a vibrant depiction of the glorified Son, raised by death-defeating power, calling all nations to enjoy the presence of the Father in the power of the Spirit? Tozer puts it this way:

"Has it ever occurred to you that one hundred pianos all tuned to the same fork are automatically tuned to each other? They are of one accord by being tuned, not to each other, but to another standard to which each one must individually bow. So one hundred worshipers met together, each one looking away to Christ, are in heart nearer to each other than they could possibly be, were they to become 'unity' conscious and turn their eyes away from God to strive for closer fellowship."[60]

We are only truly unified if our eyes are on the Lord who has united us. If we have one leader, one Lord, then we can walk and live and love in the same direction. We can sing in tune with the harmony of heaven. If we draw near to follow him as individuals, we cannot help but rub shoulders and share journeys with all the others doing the same. The truth is, when following Jesus we never walk alone. Your faith is my faith, is our faith. We should stick together.

Endnotes

47. Ephesians 4:5
48. Ephesians 1:9-11
49. Lloyd-Jones, 2003, 52
50. Luke 12:50-52
51. See John 7:43, 10:19
52. John 6:67
53. I acknowledge here subjects and viewpoints with huge theological implications and extrapolations. I want to avoid a glib or shallow treatment of such issues because the last thing we need is another superficial approach to the uniqueness of Christ, the extent of the atonement or the universality of redemption for humanity. What I share here is my own conviction, namely that we are wiser
54. Ephesians 2:6
55. Ephesians 3:9-12
56. This first took place years after Pentecost, when the church in Antioch was given this label by outsides – see Acts 11:26
57. See Acts 5:40-41
58. 1 Corinthians 11:26
59. 1 Corinthians 10:17
60. Tozer, AW, *The Pursuit of God*

6
One Spirit

We have been discovering, or rediscovering, the glorious basis of our unity: the mutual love and mysterious harmony enjoyed within the Trinity. Paul urged the Ephesian churches to make every effort to maintain the unity of the Spirit[61] because:

"...there is one body and one Spirit, just as you have been called to one glorious hope for the future."[62]

In this chapter we will be exploring further the role of the Spirit in our unity. He, the Spirit of God, is not a second-class member of the Godhead, though his work to initiate, oversee and direct God's people is too often side-lined and overlooked in today's Church. It's one of those things I feel strongly about, perhaps because of my Pentecostal heritage, but more likely because I have grown to see the Spirit's work as categorically and strategically central to the purposes of God on the earth. I hope to briefly explain, by reflecting on the last two chapters.

We, the people of God, have been invited, welcomed, adopted into the family of God and the seal of our adoption is the Spirit himself. As we read in Romans 8, Paul has in mind the Roman rite of adoption and he describes the Spirit's role as pivotal to our adoption by the Father:

"You received God's Spirit when he adopted you as his own children..." [some translators call the Spirit here the "Spirit of Adoption" or "Spirit of Sonship".] See how pivotal is his role...

"Now [because of the work of the Spirit] we call him, 'Abba, Father.' For his Spirit joins with our spirit to affirm that we are God's children. And since we are his children, we are his heirs. In fact, together with Christ we are heirs of God's glory."

For sure there is another teaching here, about the primary work of the Holy Spirit in the life of every believer. We must remember that even before anyone has spoken in tongues or prophesied, the regenerated woman or man, boy or girl, is able to utter the most profound and simple cry. It is the cry of a child to their Father:

"Daddy."

We are united as God's children by the Spirit of Adoption. He confirms our acceptance, forever, into the eternal household, the palace of the King of kings. What a basis for our harmony and what power we have available to maintain what the Father has established through the sacrifice of his Son. Can you see how this all fits together?

Furthermore, let's see in Ephesians the pivotal, dynamic role the Spirit plays in our salvation and in our unity:

"... you Gentiles have also heard the truth, the Good News that God saves you. And when you believed in Christ, he identified you as his own by giving you the Holy Spirit, whom he promised long ago. The Spirit is God's guarantee that he will give us the inheritance he promised and that he has purchased us to be his own people. He did this so we would praise and glorify him."[63]

The reception of the in-dwelling Spirit by those who believed in Jesus was (and is) proof that faith is real. The evidential presence of the Holy Spirit in other believers' lives is a uniting force across the divide of race and background. In other words, when the power of God moves into our lives, it shows (a bit like being 8-months pregnant, or deeply in love – you can't hide it).

We see this dynamic at work in the early Church, in the paradigm-shifting moment when the Gentiles were beginning to come to Christ. The Apostle Peter, a faithful Jew, is led by the Spirit into an adventure with enormous consequences. Luke tells the story so well: Peter finds himself opening the door to Cornelius and his pagan, Gentile, family as they are ushered by the Spirit into the household of the Lord. Peter is complicit in their conversion and to the outraged Jews he has to give account. How can the established church members be sure that those Gentiles can be considered "one of us"? Here is Peter's defence:

"'As I began to speak,' Peter continued, 'the Holy Spirit fell on them, just as he fell on us at the beginning. Then I thought of the Lord's words when he said, "John baptized with water, but you will be baptized with the Holy Spirit." And since God gave these Gentiles the same gift he gave us when we believed in the Lord Jesus Christ, who was I to stand in God's way?' When the others heard this, they stopped objecting and began praising God. They said, 'We can see that God has also given the Gentiles the privilege of repenting of their sins and receiving eternal life.'"[64]

I love that story and we should still love this truth: the Spirit of God seals and guarantees our adoption into the Father's family, enabling us to call him "Dad" and anoints us with power to speak the languages of heaven.

What's more, the Spirit continues, today, to animate the whole body of Christ, the breath of God still expanding in our hearts, inspiring our worship, igniting our praise. Paul prays for the Ephesian Christians:

"I pray that from his glorious, unlimited resources [the Father] will empower you with inner strength through his Spirit."[65]

Inner strength, for us all, amongst us all. You see, this is not a prayer we can simply interpret with our individualistic, consumerist world view and compare with our Buddhist friends. "Oh yeah – you've got inner strength. So do I. Peace, deep in there somewhere, yes strong. Very strong. Snap!" No, I rather think we lose the strength of Paul's whole argument if we reduce this prayer, this teaching and apply it to the faith of the individual. May I suggest the prayer is for them all, in unity, for all the believers, to receive among them, within their fellowship, a strength by God's Spirit that holds them together. For sure, every church in that era and since has needed inner strength. Resolve to stick together. Paul's prayer continues, in the plural. He is writing to a united group:

"[When you have inner strength by the Spirit] Christ will make his home in your hearts as you trust in him. Your roots will grow down into God's love and keep you strong. And may you have the power to understand, as all God's people should, how wide, how long, how high, and how deep his love is. May you experience the love of Christ, though it is too great to understand fully. Then you will be made complete with all the fullness of life and power that comes from God."[66]

What a prayer! Think about it for one more moment. How could we possibly even begin to grasp the depth, height and extent of God's love except within community? Love is relational and only makes real sense in relationship with those around us. As John said, if we're not loving others we don't truly know the love of God.[67] The completeness Paul urges them towards is that they might have a fullness of life and power that comes from the strength and dynamic of the Spirit. We are animated, brought to life, empowered, and only able to explore the fullness of God's love as the Spirit enables us all, in community.

Here is the Spirit of unity, who makes available within us and between us, the unity of the Spirit. Do we recognise his work? Can we see the evidence of his work in believers whose background and way of life we would naturally turn away from? We have one shared experience of the work of the Spirit and we share the same "glorious hope for the future" – a hope that is a gift of the Spirit within.

We could say so much more here about the edifying role of the Spirit as he gives leadership and functional gifts to the body that equip and bring maturity to the Church. Countless pages have been written on these subjects and about the fruit of the Spirit as enjoyed by, and lovingly produced in, God's people. For now, though, I think we have established firmly enough the outline of our theological basis as we explore life to the power of *one*.

Unity starts with God and will end with him in focus too. We have been united, adopted into the family of one Father, so we have to work at this because whilst you can choose your friends, you can't choose your family.[68] We have been united in our grateful follower-ship of our one Lord, saved by his blood and now obeying his heavenwards call, harmonising with the worship of heaven that extols his risen glory. We have been empowered and adopted by the work of the same one Spirit (whether Jew or Gentile) who has sealed, guaranteed, proven and evidenced among us our shared inheritance.

So if all this has been achieved, so much accomplished already, why do we keep falling out? If God has done so much to unite us, why all the discord and what can be done? These are good questions and we turn to the anatomy of unity in the next few chapters. It seems essential that we cannot "make every effort" to keep a unity we don't understand. It would be like accepting a challenge to win a game without knowing the rules; or the point of the game.

If you're still reading, I hope you will walk forward into Part 3 of this book with some fresh thoughts, and perhaps new questions, about the call to work with God in the preservation of his family's unity. We are moving steadily towards some practical, liveable principles that (if applied) will bring life and transformation, hope and fruit, to our relationships at home and at work, in our churches and between our churches too. As we continue, may the eyes of our hearts be enlightened and may our communities be blessed.

Endnotes
61. Ephesians 4:3
62. Ephesians 4:4
63. Ephesians 1:13-14
64. Acts 11:15-18
65. Ephesians 3:16
66. Ephesians 3:17-19
67. 1 John 4:20
68. You can choose to leave your family. And many do. That's why I am writing this book, to give keys for a stronger family at home, at church and in our towns and cities.

Part 3:
The Anatomy of Unity

"We belong to the same family, we are related to one another as brothers and sisters; the same blood, as it were, is coursing through our arteries and veins…"
–Martyn Lloyd-Jones

One of our favourite games to play as a family on a long journey or a New Years' Day walk (we do walk on other days of the year!) is "I'm Thinking of an Animal". You may have come across this simple time-passing game: one person starts by picturing in their mind a specific animal and then everyone else has to ask "yes" or "no" questions to discover what it is. These games have been particularly hilarious in those years when our youngest, less schooled in zoology or animal physiology and habitat, have answered a few questions wrong on the way and we end the game giving up, only to discover we were trying to picture in our mind a duck-billed platypus with six legs having babies in the Antarctic! Whilst we might have an idea of what the unity of the Spirit really is, as God intended it, we need to ask some "yes" or "no" questions.

There is much vagueness in this area of contemporary thought and practical theology in the ecumenical and "unification" movements, and amongst many people a fear of the unknown in this arena. We should be wary of rushed definitions and, from my perspective, we should be especially determined to remain faithful to the New Testament ideals of the unity of the Spirit – a unity that God asks us to maintain with every effort.

So what is it that we are expected to hold on to and what should we not pursue? If we can understand this more, if we can tell what the unity of the Spirit is and isn't, we can begin to explore the power of that unity to bless our homes, our families, our teams and workplaces, our churches and even our communities. This is surely a worthy pursuit, so stick with it!

Endnotes:
69. Lloyd-Jones, 2006, 65

7

Let's Not Go There: What Unity Isn't

"Talent perceives differences; genius, unity."
—*William Butler Yeats*

In this section we'll be looking at the body of Christ from different angles, like a sculptor forming a shape from stone. This idea brings to mind a famous (if apocryphal) anecdote:

After marvelling at Michelangelo's statue of Goliath-vanquishing David, the Pope asked the sculptor, "How do you know what to cut away?"

Michelangelo's reply? "It's simple. I just remove everything that doesn't look like David."[70]

If we are God's masterpiece, if our love-sharing, selfless unity is really one of the defining characteristics of his people, our trademark, then it must have some definition, some shape to it. In this chapter I want to suggest a few things that the unity of the Spirit is not. Let's take away some false assumptions and unhealthy pressures and see what we have left.

Uniformity

Firstly, and perhaps most importantly, the unity of the Spirit is not, and cannot be, reduced to uniformity. Whilst equal in value under God, we are not all the same in function or in strategic use, or in shape, size, approach and colour. It is self-evident all around us in creation and I don't want to patronise anyone by pointing out the inanely obvious. However, we must remember that we often work so differently to the Holy Spirit, as Lloyd-Jones explains:

"Man goes in for mass-production, and works in a mechanical manner…But when the Holy Spirit does God's work within us, it is in all cases essentially the same work, but it is always a living vital work, not mechanical and not identical in detail."[71]

However basic this principle, it is amazing how often we get this wrong. Too often we struggle with difference and are strangely comforted by sameness. The apostle Paul uses the analogy of the human body several times in his writings about the Church. It is his favourite illustration. He highlights that different parts of the body have unique, specific, valuable roles to play in the health of the whole. This is a concept we will return to repeatedly in coming chapters. For instance,

"…the body has many different parts, not just one part… If the whole body were an eye, how would you hear? Or if your whole body were an ear, how would you smell anything?"[72]

In the human body it is said that a mature adult has on average 37.2 trillion cells, of around 200 different types, and within those cell types there are around 20 different structures or organelles.[73] That's some variety! Though Paul lived a few years before Google was able to tell him that, even in his plain first century view of the wonderful, multifarious human form, a picture was painted of a church in rich variety. The Church is to reflect and celebrate the Creator's love of infinite complexity, not parasitic uniformity. You see, there are single-celled organisms in this world, "monads" they are called, and given their obvious limitations they tend towards parasitic behaviour. They sit there, suck life and nutrients from things with multiple cells and go nowhere. Before you start picturing anyone in particular (steady!) remember that there are 7.1 billion people alive today and each and every one of us has a unique DNA, an intra-nuclear fingerprint that defines our physiological uniqueness, quite apart from aspects of our personality and spirituality that genetics do not determine.

How could any organisation, any group of people, any community consisting of uniquely created, one-off individuals, produce uniformity? No thanks, we'll send that idea to Room 101.

Predictability

In a similar vein, and building on this concept, we must take away from our thinking this idea of predictability. There is too much of this in our lives, in our prayer lives, and (for sure) in our churches.

Some have argued that only atheism offers a predictable universe, because it is based on natural laws that are absolute and unchangeable.[74] The believer's world runs according to the commands of God, not just the laws of nature (which he himself defines). Our lives are defined by God's consistency of nature (his love and faithfulness), not his predictability.

As Isaiah celebrated in his prophetic poem, *"Truly, O God of Israel, our Saviour, you work in mysterious ways…"*[75]

He always has, and always will. Our God is mysterious, unaccountable to us, moving and shaping and building in ways for his own good pleasure. In explaining the mysterious means by which a human can be born again of the Spirit, in John 3 Jesus uses the words for "wind" and "Spirit" interchangeably. Neither the wind nor the Spirit respond to our direction: *"The wind blows wherever it wants."*[76]

Applying this to our unity as the people of the Spirit then, we should recognise this will rarely produce in us, or through us, predictability. We should aspire to reflect God's consistency of character but not limit ourselves to a dull, uniform predictability. What does this mean? This is not necessarily doing away with traditions or patterns of worship, but neither should it become a blind pursuit of the predictable and predetermined; unity should celebrate the new while honouring the established.

I was discussing this recently with a respected New Testament author (and my favourite lecturer), Dr Conrad Gempf. We were musing over the harmonic and rhythmic aspects of Christian unity and wondering if the pursuit of this unity is altogether different from orchestrating things in unison. Is our aim a case of getting everyone in the Church to "sing from the same songsheet"[77] where the same words at the same time are sung in the same way? Is this a picture of what we are meant to make every effort to maintain?

The unity of the Spirit is dynamic, ever-changing, moving, reflecting his personhood as the life-force of creation, the initiator of new. Predictable? Not so sure.

Ambiguity

We have already touched on this in chapter 5 when we considered the uniqueness of Christ and the challenge to be united in our conviction of who he is. There is no faith if there is no Christ and there is only one of him. Typically, Martyn Lloyd-Jones raises his "banner of Truth" to underline a fundamental assertion that we are united not out a spirit of friendship, but by the Spirit of God:

"Paul is not writing about the manifestation of some human spirit of friendship, he is not thinking in terms of the so-called public-school spirit, or the cricket-team spirit, or that of the football team. It is a capital S, it is The Holy Spirit."[78]

In the pluralistic world we work out our faith in, the idea of being united in the Spirit, and by Truth, a personal Truth, is far from popular. Even as you read this, you may be wondering how we can stick together if we don't agree about the person, work, and uniqueness of Christ? I guess that is my point. Unity and ambiguity cannot co-exist. If we are unclear about who and what unites us, we have no unity. What we have may be a sense of common humanity, or of congeniality, or even very deep friendship and loyalty. But what we are looking at is deeper, more profound than all of these things.

Imagine the scene, two teams are about to emerge from the changing rooms ready for the big match. The crowd go crazy and from different ends of the stadium, standing to their feet, they cheer: "Come on you blues", "Come on you reds!" The teams come onto the pitch, but something is wrong. Every player is wearing a different colour shirt. Who is on which team? How can they possibly play together if their team colours are ambiguous?

Now I know I said our unity is not uniformity, but in tension with this truth, neither can we be united by vague, wishy-washy ambiguity. The fear of defining what unites would be like building a house of bricks with no mortar, and to me some aspects of the ecumenical movement veer dangerously towards bland ambiguity. I believe the unity of the Spirit is strong and not weak, clear and not vague, in tune with the Godhead not discordant and undefined.

Symmetry

From an early age I loved to draw, lay out items on a page, design new typefaces, and this love ultimately grew into an expertise in graphic design. I was so grateful when the GCSE curriculum was introduced to allow so much page layout in the coursework. I swear it was my desktop publishing skills that got me my "A" grade in geography! In fact, the most positive comment the aforementioned Dr Gempf made on my first essay assignment at London School of Theology was about the typography on the cover! All this to introduce another element I don't think we should look for in Christian unity: symmetry.

Symmetry; balanced arrangement: it is a strength in wheel design, but often a weakness in art. It is a life-saver in road design, but can stifle growth in an organisation. I think we are too often looking for people, churches, teams, communities, to achieve some form of symmetry and I am not sure that strikes a chord with the unity of the Spirit.

When I was studying graphic design at Norwich Art College I was first introduced to the Golden Section, also known as (please note) "the Divine Proportion". Without going into too much detail, suffice to say it is the application of a mathematical formula that results in the Fibonacci sequence of numbers. When applied to visual and structural composition and proportion, it produces a spiral that is mysteriously found in some of the most beautiful, pleasing-to-the-eye forms in creation. Picture in your mind a simple sea shell and you'll instantly get what I mean. The Golden Section has been discovered in works of art and architecture, often by design but also often by "mistake". This asymmetrical composition, influential in the simpler "rule of thirds" principle, pleases the eye despite its imbalance and maybe because of it. It creates momentum and enhances scale.

Now I don't want to draw too fine a point on this, but I would suggest that bilateral symmetry, perfect balance, mirror images, exact copies, are fine for works of engineering but not our aim when working with people. Or building with people. The last thing we all need is to be balanced and the last thing the Spirit (who created us all uniquely) wants is for his Church to look and feel the same whichever way we look at it.

There is something glorious about the imbalance of the Church, isn't there? When we step back and take a look at even our own families, our own teams and churches, what we see is a more a work of art than a piece of engineering. Thank God for that.

Superiority

Paul the apostle makes it clear in his writings: there is no room for arrogance or self-importance in the Church of Jesus Christ. This new community of faith is now, in very essence, the body of Christ on the earth. We are his hands and feet:

> *"Yes, there are many parts, but only one body. The eye can never say to the hand, 'I don't need you.' The head can't say to the feet, 'I don't need you.'"*[79]

All it takes is a bit of success, a touch of acclaim or an overdose of affirmation and we can take flight on the wings of our own superiority. This is anathema to the unity of the Spirit. It is cancerous within families, devastating in churches, and between churches it is too common by far. Pride puffs us up, strokes our egos, inflates our sense of worth and, when fuelled with the tangible fruit of numerical growth or increased popularity, it tears down the very unity we have been called to maintain.

Let's not go to that place where a few people, even churches, claim superiority; where denominational pride causes some to look down on others saying, "We don't need you." This understandable attitude flies in the face of God's purposes. It supposes that we can easily compare one part of the body to the other when they play a different role altogether. This is Paul's concern and it should be ours. He wrote to the church in Rome:

"I give each of you this warning: Don't think you are better than you really are. Be honest in your evaluation of yourselves, measuring yourselves by the faith God has given us."[80]

Maintaining the unity of the Spirit requires us to look down on others no longer.

Inferiority

The other side to this comparison coin is just as important. If we are to make every effort to keep the unity of the Spirit we will cheerfully, gratefully embrace our own greatness in God's eyes. It is a sign of insecurity, of immaturity, to fail to see ourselves as God sees us.

In the context of the earlier passage we read from 1 Corinthians, *"If the foot says, 'I am not a part of the body because I am not a hand,' that does not make it any less a part of the body. And if the ear says, 'I am not part of the body because I am not an eye,' would that make it any less a part of the body?"[81]*

We are urged here to stop excluding ourselves with a complex of inferiority. We must stop counting ourselves out when God counts us in! Some cultures are renowned for their self-hating, self-deprecating nature, looking at other people, even other nations, and wallowing in inferiority and self pity. This will not wash with the Spirit of God who has bestowed upon followers of Christ gifts of his own choosing. He has gifted some more than others, and all of us uniquely, and our perspective is often wrong when comparing what we see. *"In fact, some parts of the body that seem weakest and least important are actually the most necessary."*[82]

When working with other churches in Watford, from time to time I have heard a whiff of this inferiority, often expressed by church leaders in those insecure moments of a conversation. You know, when someone tells you of their success, or of something good that is happening in their community. In those awkward moments, I have heard leaders say things like, "At least you're doing something worthwhile – we're just waiting for retirement!" Or, "We might as well close our doors and give up if you're doing that." Insecurity tempts us all to despair in different times of our lives, but let's resist it. The body of Christ requires and needs every part to do its own special work,[83] and in the end, even in our towns and cities, the most necessary expression of the church may not in fact be the one we would value the most. We'll explore that more in a later chapter. I trust we get this simple point: the unity of the Spirit is not compatible with self-pity, false humility or inferiority. Every part of the body has a special place.

Endnotes

70. http://www.lifeclever.com/what-michelangelo-can-teach-you-about-good-design/
71. Lloyd-Jones, 2006, 60
72. 1 Corinthians 12:14, 17
73. http://www.smithsonianmag.com/smart-news/there-are-372-trillion-cells-in-your-body-4941473 and http://sciencenetlinks.com/student-teacher-sheets/cells-your-body/
74. http://carm.org/only-atheism-offers-predictable-universe

75. Isaiah 45:15
76. John 3:8
77. I mean, projector screen.
78. Lloyd-Jones, 1980, 37
79. 1 Corinthians 11:20
80. Romans 12:3
81. 1 Corinthians 12:15-16
82. 1 Corinthians 12:22
83. Ephesians 4:16

8
The Real Thing:
What Unity Is

"The essence of the beautiful is unity in variety."
– W. Somerset Maugham

I feel privileged to be living in a town like Watford and serving alongside some incredible men and women of God. Not least those we serve alongside in Wellspring Church, volunteer leaders and staff members. On an even deeper level than that, there have been profound moments when my wife Helen and I have tasted and seen something of the beauty of unity in Christ.[84] It is like a symphony, an almost indescribable dynamic when hearts and minds and efforts combine in such a way that heaven seems to respond with a smile, and the fruit is transformation in the lives of others.

In the autumn of 2014 we were grateful to host an evangelist friend, Mark Ritchie, to spend 10 days in Watford. He travelled from one venue to another (churches and community centres), telling stories and explaining the gospel in a town-wide outreach under the banner of Christians Across Watford. We saw over

1,000 people attend one of those events and many people respond to the gospel in a significant way. In the middle of that mission week there was a moment, a leaders' breakfast in fact, when alongside the taste of fresh bread and sausages we tasted the unity of the Spirit. Whilst Mark was our guest speaker, God showed up in a simple, beautiful way. Around a common table, a dozen or so leaders laughed, prayed, shared, listened and simply "dwelt" together in an atmosphere of warmth and sincerity and in the context of shared mission and united purpose. The sense of God's presence that Wednesday morning at St Mary's is hard to describe. We felt the Father's smile, because some of the ingredients we are talking about here were present in that gathering, as they have been before and as we hope to experience more often.

So in our teams and towns, churches and homes, what does the unity of the Spirit look like? Here are some ideas.

Diversity

We have already touched on this and it is an essential ingredient of true togetherness. We must celebrate our differences. There is such variety in creation, in the human race, in the shapes of clouds over the Alps and the colours of tropical fish in the Red Sea. We look at these things and marvel at DNA, and watch a crowd of thousands wondering how God could love us all, and we find ourselves lost in worship. As a sign of God's handiwork, an expression of his own loving togetherness, we celebrate the diversity we see.

Until we have to live with difference.

In Chief Rabbi Jonathan Sacks' compelling classic, *The Dignity of Difference*, he reflects on an ancient Jewish prayer, explaining:

"Normally we thank God for what we have, not what we lack:

for our gifts, not our deficiencies. The explanation is that if each of us lacked nothing, we would never need anyone else. We would be solitaries, complete in ourselves. The very fact that we are different means what I lack, someone else has, and what someone else lacks, I have."[85]

As Sacks also explains,

"The God of Abraham teaches a more complex truth than simple oppositions... We are particular and universal, the same [in our humanity] and different... Just as a loving parent is pained by sibling rivalry, so God asks us, his children, not to fight or seek to dominate one another. God, author of diversity, is the unifying presence within diversity."[86]

There is great beauty in our difference and the unity of God's Spirit is found not in homogeny but rather rich variety.

We will apply this principle more fully in a later chapter, but it is worth pausing for a moment and asking for wisdom to see how this theory can apply to our own lives and relationships. With the Babel epic still in mind, we can recall how the covenant made with Abraham was not a promise to do away with linguistic or cultural diversity, to subsume all nations into a mono-nation. Rather, the promise was that all nations, all other nations would be blessed through his faithful offspring. Many centuries later, on the day of Pentecost when the Holy Spirit was poured on the believers in the Upper Room, the manifestation of God's power was that the praises of the One True God were heard and understood in the different languages of the populace. The diversity of language on those streets was not done away with, it was instead, bridged, for the glory of God.

If we are to build homes and teams and churches that cause heaven to smile with the Father's pleasure, we must hold on to our diversity, maintain our differences, even celebrating others' uniqueness with heartfelt joy.

Harmony

The musical analogy of unity is such a helpful one. There are moments in music when the hearer (or indeed the musician) is taken to another place. We tune into something of heavenly bliss. We are all different (see above!) so for some these ecstatic moments are found in the accord of a choir, a barbershop quartet or an operatic chorus. For others it is the crescendo of a symphony orchestra, the moment of syncopation in improvised jazz, or the spontaneous choral takeover amongst thousands at a rock concert. That moment, that spine-tingling dynamic, is what I mean by harmony.

It is in the very nature of God to bring each of us together, his family, his children, and encourage in us a full and heartfelt expression of our worship to him. Not so that we sound the same, but so our lives and hearts resonate with heaven and harmony is achieved. Our dear friend and powerfully anointed worship pastor Ben Kirk once said, "No one can sing like you can, no one can play the instrument of your soul or offer your worship." It's not a compliment (he has heard me sing!), it is a profound truth: we bring our own lives as an instrument to be combined with others.

The musical analogy could be taken too far, but there is one more aspect of this we should consider. Dr Gempf asked me if I knew about sympathetic vibrations. He wasn't inviting me to a New Age festival (I don't think!). What we discussed was the audial dynamic that takes place when instruments respond to each other.

Imagine the scene: you take an amplifier into Wembley Music

Centre where drum kits fill rooms and guitars line the walls. You plug your MP3 player into the amplifier and turn it up. Loud. It is Vivaldi's Four Seasons. As the violin dances through the season of "Spring" with delicacy and grace, the Gibson electric guitars (favourites of heavy metal bands) start to vibrate along the side of the room; the snare drums and cymbals start to shake. Diverse and different instruments join in with Vivaldi's concerto. If you turn up the volume, you get sympathetic vibrations. Perhaps there is something in this for us to consider: the potential in our own lives and organisations for a resonance of diversity in harmony.

As we keep the unity of the Spirit, straining to maintain it, I pray there will be more and more moments of heaven's harmony in our communities. This will happen when churches and individuals, with diverse and personal qualities, turn up their volume, listen and respond, and in celebration of rich variety, bring glory to the Spirit who calls the tune.

Dignity

The "body" imagery of the united Church, so rich in depth and so clear in application, points us to our third ingredient for the real unity of the Spirit: dignity. I remember as a child looking through illustrated encyclopaedias and biology textbooks and sniggering, embarrassed at the diagrams and photographs of naked people. As for the diagrams under Reproduction... yuck! There are some parts of the human anatomy that are, let's face it, just weird.

The apostle Paul refers to our weird bits, our private parts, in his epistle to the Corinthians:

> *"...the parts we regard as less honourable are those we clothe with the greatest care. So we carefully protect those parts that should not be seen, while the more honourable parts do not require this*

special care. So God has put the body together such that extra honour and care are given to those parts that have less dignity. This makes for harmony [unity] among the members, so that all the members care for each other."[87]

So he doesn't draw them a diagram, but the apostle is calling the believers to provide and protect the dignity of every member of their church (including the most vulnerable). So too should we. One of the hallmarks of the early Church was their Spirit-enabled inclusion of those society had rejected. Widows were cared for, provided for, welcomed in and given an equal place around the Lord's table; divorcees and ex-prostitutes, children and lepers, Jews and Gentiles, slaves and masters, all afforded dignity in the community of Christ.

"Christians offered both food and family. They talked of themselves as a social unit, as a family, as brother and sister. Where the Roman world praised and rewarded the powerful and the wealthy and the well born, the Christians provided a place for the weak and the poor and the lowest of the low."[88]

Whilst we could take a rosy view of those early days in the Church, we can tell from the book of Acts and the apostolic letters we've read that division and humiliation knocked constantly at the doors of their gatherings. Just like today. Factions and fractures emerge early in church history and they have threatened every Christian community since. What the devil of division loves to do is to steal people's dignity, to humiliate, expose, render helpless and vulnerable, and rob our desire as a community to respond to the shame and brokenness of others with grace.

The Spirit of unity is the Spirit of dignity. Isaiah prophesied to a coldly religious Israel about God's chosen fast, the Lord's preferred form of sacrificial worship:

"This is the kind of fasting I want:
Free those who are wrongly imprisoned;
lighten the burden of those who work for you.
Let the oppressed go free,
and remove the chains that bind people.
Share your food with the hungry,
and give shelter to the homeless.
Give clothes to those who need them,
and do not hide from relatives who need your help."[89]

This same idea is reiterated by Jesus as he warns his followers of the dangers of paying lip-service to the values of his new kingdom. In Matthew 25 he tells a parable of a King returning to commend those who lived by his standard. Their integrity is commended because they invited the stranger in, clothed the naked, cared for the sick, and visited the prisoner.[90] This is the essence of our commission as Christ's followers and without doubt must be an ingredient of the Spirit's unity.

What would this look like in your team, in your church?

Would the uniting Spirit of dignity refuse to humiliate the weak or shame the struggling, and would we cooperate with him to follow suit?

In taking a fresh look at the anatomy of Christian unity, we need to go beyond just recognising what it is and isn't. Our analysis must not be remote or passive. The call of the Spirit to make every effort in maintaining unity requires us to explore what it will take, what it will cost. It is to this we will turn next.

Endnotes
84. I'll spare you the blushes.
85. Sacks, J, 2003, 100, with credit given to Joshua Rowe
86. Ibid., 56

87. 1 Corinthians 12:23-25
88. Park, Nick, Kingdom of Fools, 2012, 103
89.Isaiah 58:6-7
90. Matthew 25:34-40

9
Count The Cost:
What Unity Requires of Us

"Where there is unity there is always victory."
–Publilius Syrus

Our eldest daughter Bethany is an excellent artist. She loves to draw and paint, and as she is progressing through her Fine Art A level, every piece she produces takes the quality of her work to another level. It's an exciting thing to see and my artistic ability to help her is fast becoming redundant. She is overtaking me in her gift. Recently she was taken by her grandmother to an exhibition at the V&A Museum in London of work by the great eighteen/nineteenth century landscape artist, John Constable. The exhibition was entitled "The Making of a Master" and Bethany was enthralled by what she saw. On display were, of course, the vast 2-metre canvases of oil paintings such as *The Haywain* and *The Leaping Horse*.

However, this exhibition showed the extensive process of planning, preparation and sketching that was involved in producing these stunning, moving masterpieces. In fact,

Constable's genius was the result of months and years of prior planning and learning from other artists.

All this is to say that, having painted a picture of unified diversity, replete with dignity and harmony and free from such things as a uniformed predictability, ambiguity and the fruits of comparison, we must count the cost. We must plan, prepare and consider what it is going to take.

You see, I wholeheartedly believe your relationships could be stronger. I believe your home could be more united. If you are married, your marriage can be stronger. Beyond that, it is my conviction that there are principles and practices being discussed here that could see stronger bonds formed between you and your colleagues at work, in your team, across your church and even amongst the Christian community where you live. These are not new principles, I haven't discovered an elixir. However, the reason we are on this journey (and the reason you're still reading at this point) is because we know we have so much to learn about the unity of the Spirit. We know we haven't made every effort to stay united with others in Christ and we have seen and felt the pain of the division that results.

So, what is "every effort"? What is the cost of unity's blessing? Here are some thoughts…

Humility

The first and most obvious quality we must foster is humility. In his challenging letter to the Ephesians, Paul writes:

"Therefore I, a prisoner for serving the Lord, beg you to lead a life worthy of your calling, for you have been called by God. Always be humble and gentle. Be patient with each other, making allowance for each other's faults because of your love."[91]

Francis Foulkes points out that these verses outline a four-dimensional quality to Christian community – characteristics that can apply to individuals but also organisations: *lowliness, meekness, longsuffering* and *forbearance*. At first glance these words sound weak until we remember the example of Christ. In the Greek world, Foulkes highlights, *"'the fullness of life... left no room for humility.' In Christ lowliness becomes a virtue."*[92] It was in the life, example and sacrifice of Jesus that we see humility introduced as a high value in society, a new standard for a new community.

A plain reading of the gospel accounts reveals Jesus as a working man, a builder, of significant strength (both physical and mental), focus and discipline, infinite grace and breath-taking fortitude. To see what he saw, learn what he learned, and undertake the mission he was sent to complete, required the perfect balance of forbearance and lowliness. Jesus is the clear picture of humility, true humility. It is the utter confidence in who you are (we see this in Jesus' self-awareness) and the conscious decision to put others first (supremely expressed on Calvary's cross). In his book *Mere Christianity*, C S Lewis explains, *"True humility is not thinking less of yourself; it is thinking of yourself less."*

For our purposes in building communities of unity, the application is clear and straightforward in principle, and yet agonising in its demands. Much of the effort required to keep the unity of the Spirit is about cooperating with him as he gives us a right view of ourselves (lifting our heads from inferiority and correcting our arrogance), but then the Sprit also gives us something more important to focus our attention on: *others*.

To the church in Philippi:

"Is there any encouragement from belonging to Christ? Any comfort from his love? Any fellowship together in the Spirit? Are your hearts tender and compassionate? Then make me truly happy by agreeing wholeheartedly with each other, loving one another, and working together with one mind and purpose.

Don't be selfish; don't try to impress others. Be humble, thinking of others as better than yourselves. Don't look out only for your own interests, but take an interest in others, too."[93]

In this powerful missive from the apostle Paul, he follows this challenge with a poem of the *kenosis*, the self-emptying sacrifice of Christ for our sakes. A united community (a family sticking together, for that matter) is described so beautifully here: a fellowship of tenderness and compassion, wholehearted agreement, selflessness; a people who see the beauty, the dignity, the infinite value of those around them. What a stunning thought and what a vision for God's people: a family of faith where people look out for others' interests as well as their own. Wouldn't you love your church to be described in such a way? Have you experienced this before? If you have, you will know there is a cost to building such unity. It requires a willing, humble turning away from self-obsession.

Much is being said and written about the "selfie generation" where narcissism has been digitised and normalised. With the camera turned away from the world's most beautiful landmarks, instead of publishing the beauty we see before us, we are posting on the Internet photos of ourselves. We Instagram with filters and trash the parts we want to hide, displaying forever the projection of us we are happy for people to see. We are a generation that can, and does, crop out our weaknesses and changes the lighting on our profile, until what is seen is acceptable to the "others" that matter. And the others will compare and comment and add that image to the grid of their own self-reference. This is the way our world is now. It is in this context that Jesus' example of selfless humility challenges us to the core. It is into today's society that we accept Paul's call to build communities of true humility, putting others first and following the example of Christ.

Humility requires us to take an honest look at ourselves, acknowledging our strengths and weaknesses and then, crucially, a conscious decision to overlook ourselves and focus instead on others. This is the cost of unity.

Generosity

There are some people we meet that just lift us by their presence. We feel bigger and better whenever we come across them. Perhaps you have people in your life that build you up in this way? For the Roberts family one of those truly uplifting people is a spiritual father, Ron Corzine. He exemplifies, for me, a generous spirit. The cost of building communities of genuine unity is the decision to live lives that consciously bless others, through words and deeds, leaving a deposit at every opportunity.

Ron and his wife Anne are some of the most fun people to be around. They offer warm hospitality and they have planted churches that celebrate life in the love of God and the enjoyment of his presence.

By my reckoning, this is not an accident or just a supernatural gift of God's grace. I can see in Ron's own life and ministry an absolute determination to be generous to others. To give them the benefit of the doubt. To treat volunteers and staff well, to pay them properly, to build Christian community inspired by the generosity of God and not the tight-fistedness of selfish humanity.

Unity-keeping is costly and it requires intentional generosity.

Is this about money? Not really, although when we are cheap in our thinking towards others and small-minded in relationships, we will be stingy with our cash. If we are to consider others better than ourselves, we will be generous with giving our time and resources to help them grow. Generosity will cost us our preferences and our comfort. We won't always get our way; we may even see others succeed in our stead and have to choose to celebrate when they do.

Our son, David, is as naturally competitive as his father. Lord, help him! He will race anyone to be first back to the car. He loves beating me on *FIFA 15* and struggles not to sulk if he loses. Whatever the game, or the contest, he often values winning more than playing the game. In my own immaturity, I resonate with that view on life! Nevertheless, when playing the board game *Monopoly*, David seems to lose perspective on the aim of the game quite quickly. Maybe this is because it's almost impossible to beat our middle daughter Hannah in this land-grabbing game of territorial domination. She's a tycoon in the making (or maybe she wins because she's always the banker!) Her brother, however, instead of stockpiling cash or even property, early on in a game will be overcome by waves of compassion and sympathy and start giving away his notes and even entering into loss-making negotiations for Regent Street to help an opponent get all the green ones. It's funny, so endearing, and reminds me of the generosity that builds relationships.

As we have already seen, the Christian Church faced opposition and temptation from the outset. The work of the Holy Spirit, though, was producing amongst this tiny community of Christ-followers, some unique, heavenly qualities. The beginning of a new kingdom based on Jesus' teaching and example. Luke describes the scene:

"All the believers were united in heart and mind. And they felt that what they owned was not their own, so they shared everything they had. The apostles testified powerfully to the resurrection of the Lord Jesus, and God's great blessing was upon them all. There were no needy people among them, because those who owned land or houses would sell them and bring the money to the apostles to give to those in need."[94]

Generosity: unity requires it from us all. We cannot stick together if we will not share what we have. The love of God is a selfless, giving, generous love. When this love is shed abroad in our hearts and demonstrated in our lives, true and lasting communities can be built. What's more, as unified communities of faith and selfless love continually experience and exude the health and life of the King, those around cannot help but receive some benefits. We will explore this further in the next section. There is exponential potential in seeing communities transformed with God's love when the Church of Christ functions in mutual generosity and enjoys the unity of the Spirit.

We are called by God to follow in the footsteps of Christ and throw our all into seeing his kingdom come on the earth. This is our Great Commission. We must recognise this is intrinsically a team effort because it takes a community to change communities. God's love, as we have shown, doesn't make sense without relationship. His love cannot be fully experienced in isolation nor grasped outside of community. The invitation in Ephesians 1 to know (encounter) the love of God in Christ is a plea to his collective, to his followers. As such, in pursuit of this collective Commission, we must generously contribute all we can to its completion. Missions always cost. They need time, expertise and money. Communal causes demand and require commitment and sacrifice, and the more members who participate in this self-giving, the more possible success becomes.

The unity of the Spirit is made more possible when an attitude, an atmosphere, of generosity is encouraged. With our determination and cooperation, our homes and our churches can become those places of warmth and open-handedness we and others enjoy. Lord, help us.

Maturity

Dealing with difference, dialogue and disagreement is (to say the least), difficult. We will look in future chapters at some aspects of these struggles and how we face them in different spheres, but we must recognise the costly call of God to become mature. To grow up. So many times in these last two decades of Christian leadership I have wanted to shout, "Grow up, will you!"

Most often I have been looking in the mirror, disgusted and frustrated by my own insecurity, immaturity and selfishness. "Grow up, you idiot!" Flummoxed by an off-the cuff remark that I should brush off; dismayed because something I planned didn't work first time; simple, small, stupid things have exposed the childish ways within.

At other times (in one case I remember reaching boiling point while counselling a 70-year-old to recognise his adolescent behaviour), I have been appalled by the immaturity of those seeking wise counsel but lacking any determination to change their ways. Once, our friend Ron Corzine wisely refused to welcome into his office a church member, asking his secretary to ask the needy parishioner if they had put into action the advice given by Pastor Ron in their previous encounter. "They haven't done what we agreed they would? Tell them to come back when they have!" Love that. It is a pastoral approach that will not leave immaturity unchallenged.

It is this call, this invitation, to grow to maturity that runs like a sliver thread through Ephesians. In fact, unity and maturity are intrinsically linked. He explains here the purpose and place of leadership gifts in the church:

"Now these are the gifts Christ gave to the church: the apostles, the prophets, the evangelists, and the pastors and teachers. Their responsibility is to equip God's people to do his work and build up the church, the body of Christ. This will continue until we all come to such unity in our faith and knowledge of God's Son that we will be mature in the Lord, measuring up to the full and complete standard of Christ."[95]

Leaders and members of the body of Christ are charged here to grow, to equip and be equipped, to do works of service, to continue (persist) with this glorious goal in mind: to be united in faith and mature in the Lord. John Stott points out that this is not just about personal, individual maturity, but the maturing of the "one new man" described in Ephesians 2:15.[96] We are called, urged, to mature as individuals, and also as a new community.

What is that cost? What does maturity require? Surely it is like the price of physical fitness and the cost of staying healthy. It is the pain of exercising because you want to stay in good shape and not forsaking discipline because it hurts. Maturity is the result of accepting we get things wrong and deciding to enjoy learning from others. Maturity comes from reflecting on failures and celebrating successes, even those of others. What's more, maturity comes from arguing well and genuinely listening to opposing views.

Jewish leader Jonathan Sacks lays out this challenge in much of his writing: the challenge to engage in genuine conversation. His wide-reaching call is to people of all faiths and none to come together in conversation to "prevent a global age becoming the scene of intermittent but destructive wars". It is a noble aim and his grasp of the complexities of entering into mature discussion across faiths and worldviews are worth folding into the mix of our thinking here:

"[we] must learn to listen and be prepared to be surprised by others. We must make ourselves open to their stories, which may profoundly conflict with ours. We must even, at times, be ready to hear of their pain, humiliation and resentment and discover that their image of us is anything but our image of ourselves... We must learn the art of conversation... letting our world be enlarged by the presence of others who think, act, and interpret reality in ways radically different from our own."[97]

There is so much to chew over in the breadth of this challenge and I have found the Chief Rabbi's teaching refreshingly uncomfortable in considering my own dealings with those of other faiths. Nonetheless, his exploration of the value of conversation, of listening carefully to those not like us, is a vital ingredient to our maturity as members of God's family.

Immaturity is uncomfortable with tension and prefers naiveté. We would rather stick to ideas and opinions that reinforce our (often simplistic, untested) beliefs and conceptions. I fear much of the time, in our childishness, we consciously avoid the pain and discomfort of other-awareness. Infants are kept in the dark about wars in the world, the actual truth about the Tooth Fairy, and who really puts the presents under the Christmas tree. Immature minds and hearts prefer fantasy to reality. We are all the time building a worldview, seeking to make sense of the world and how it works. We wrongly presume that exposure to opposing viewpoints will upset our construction project, even destroy what we have built. I guess in the short term, as we build, we may need to re-think and reconfigure our conceptions in light of what we learn. We'll need to discard as well as add, destroy as well as build up. But this is nothing to be afraid of. The result will be more rigorous.

I see this challenge to honest, deep conversation, as an essential ingredient to our maturity as Christian communities, too. It is important in our homes, teams and churches. It is foundational in building unity across denominational divides. The idealist in me (you may have picked up this tendency so far!) is determined to see richer, deeper relationships built on substance and not superficiality, confidence and not ignorance. It's not funny, how we don't talk anymore. The tragic evidence is plain to see from the first century until now. Paul rebukes the Corinthian churches for dividing over whose nuance of Christian teaching they preferred. Some followed Apollos and others Paul[98] and the embryonic separation of Christ-followers into denominations began. Didn't take long, did it?

Making every effort, straining, pushing on, opening minds and reordering our lives to involve and include others, is a call to maturity. Painful, costly, uncomfortable conversations lie ahead but they will reap among us a unity that blesses those around us. Our vision is the kingdom of heaven expressed in fullness on earth; the radiant Church as a bride prepared and ready for the bridegroom to return. It's time for us to grow up.

Tenacity

As we consider the great cost of our pursuit, to unite disparate and diverse people into a collegiate, harmonised community, we should acknowledge a fourth and important quality this pursuit will demand of us: *tenacity.* Perseverance.

When Paul talks about making every effort, part of us instinctively knows this is going to involve some grind. Like a bricklayer starting a day's work, at a dry pallet of blocks on the ground, the plans in his hand, and the ladder inviting him two storeys up. This is going to require some work. Hard work. Yet as we think of this analogy, we are so grateful for the tenacity of the builders who built our houses, the teachers who finished their studies, the doctors who finished their training and the fathers who stayed faithful to our mothers. If you have been a recipient of such a blessing, think again at just how costly it is to finish anything worthwhile.

Paul uses Jesus as our perfect example of this tenacity. We stand acceptable in the presence of a holy God because Jesus finished his mission. He persevered through the pain and agony of all our shame and punishment, through to the other side of winning us into the household of heaven:

> *"Therefore, since we have been made right in God's sight by faith, we have peace with God because of what Jesus Christ our Lord has done for us. Because of our faith, Christ has brought us into this place of undeserved privilege where we now stand, and we confidently and joyfully look forward to sharing God's glory.*
>
> *We can rejoice, too, when we run into problems and trials, for we know that they help us develop endurance. And endurance develops strength of character, and character strengthens our confident hope of salvation. And this hope will not lead to disappointment..."*[99]

If we are to build communities of genuine unity, if we are to overcome divisions and learn to celebrate others' strengths in acknowledgment of our own weaknesses, there will be a load to carry and a demanding plan to fulfil. If we take these verses written to the Romans and apply them to our homes and our churches, we are spurred on all the more. This is a collective call for the Church to endure, to joyfully persevere because of our confident hope in the glory of heaven. It's going to be hard work, but we are building a palace on earth for the greatest King.

So far we have heard the ancient cry of the scriptures for God's new community to bless all nations. We have seen the basis of this is the unity of the Trinity: one Father, one Lord, one Spirit. In this third part of our journey we have sketched the anatomy of a united body, a harmonious Church, recognising what this includes and precludes, and what it will cost. In the final section of this book we will begin to get practical and explore what all this will mean in different aspects of our lives. We will see the power of one at work and dream in more vivid detail of a world kissed by the citizens of heaven who refuse to be divided, at home and beyond.

Endnotes
91. Ephesians 4:1-2
92. Foulkes here is quoting Robinson – see Foulkes, F, Ephesians, 108f
93. Philippians 2:1-4
94. Acts 4:32-35
95. Ephesians 4:11-13
96. Stott, J, 1991, 170
97. Sacks, J, 2003, 22f
98. See 1 Corinthians 3
99. Romans 5:1-4a

Part 3:
The Power of One

This section will bring all the previous thoughts and concepts into sharp focus on a number of levels, from how we deal with relationship breakdown that damages our unity in the home, through concentric spheres to our hopes for the role of the Church in the nations as God's new community. As stated at the beginning of this exploration, the purpose of this book is not to prescribe a magic formula or offer glib solutions to complex problems. I can make no claim to the discovery of a miracle drug to fix society's ills or offer a 5-step process to healing every hurt. What I do know, and a conviction I do carry, is that you and I can cooperate with the Holy Spirit and be part of the answer to Jesus's prayer for oneness amongst his followers. We are those followers, and as such, we should read his apostles' words, look at the division around us, and be compelled to respond with determination. We cannot turn a blind eye to this commission. There are things we can do, atmospheres we can create. There are skills we can foster and cultural qualities we can grow. So we must.

In the coming chapters we will see the power of this oneness brought to bear where it matters most: in the relationships that matter. We'll start with some of the most important relational coaching we have ever received, namely the invitation to embrace conflict with maturity and honesty, and with the integrity of the community in focus. Then we'll follow Paul's example in Ephesians, who starts his letter with overarching principles and then applies them to the nitty-gritty of daily interaction. All along we are building up to an honest, and hopefully helpful, discussion of how we can interact across towns and cities as churches and Christian communities, with a view of bringing them blessing.

10
The Art of Disagreement

*"You don't get unity by ignoring
the questions that have to be faced."*
–Jay Weatherill

The problem with everyone else in this world is that they don't think like me. It's profoundly frustrating, infuriating when all the others don't know what I want, when I want it. Instead of putting me first, letting me have my way, and living their lives for my satisfaction, and with the same perspective on the world around us, they choose to differ because they just can't help it. Some beg to differ, obstinately refusing to see things my way. Others just differ, it seems, for the fun of it. The upshot of all this is a minefield of conflict. We are facing the prospect of a lifetime of inevitable confrontation. As John Ortberg puts it, we are like porcupines trying to embrace. The closer we get, the more painful it is. Awkward.

"Our task is to create little islands of shalom in a sea of isolation. It's time to pull in your quills and start dancing."[100]

If we throw into this mix our propensity to mess things up, to sin,[101] to hurt those we love, and do damage to those we hate, we identify massive barriers to ever building community. You don't need me to point out just what a bad job we have done over the millennia, around the world, of building unified, Christ-centred, dignity-covering, genuine communities.

It call comes down to this: *disagreement.*

We must learn from the Master, Jesus, how to have a full-on disagreement. How to handle hurt and how to protect the integrity of a community (a team, a family) without sweeping the toxic dirt under the proverbial carpet. Sitting at the feet of our Lord, we expect him perhaps to tell us another parable, to spin us a yarn that we will have to disentangle to get the meaning; like the parable of the sower, or the one about Lazarus and the fiery prison. Instead, as we turn to Matthew 18 we turn to some of the most direct teaching of Jesus in the gospels. It is the nearest he gets to displaying a PowerPoint with a flowchart. Take a look at this:

> *"If another believer sins against you, go privately and point out the offence. If the other person listens and confesses it, you have won that person back. But if you are unsuccessful, take one or two others with you and go back again, so that everything you say may be confirmed by two or three witnesses. If the person still refuses to listen, take your case to the church. Then if he or she won't accept the church's decision, treat that person as a pagan or a corrupt tax collector."[102]*

We have been teaching this passage in Wellspring Church for years as a foundational practice in our church family. Why? Because we want to build a stronger community and we know this can only happen when we master the art of disagreement.

As we unpack this teaching and look at the fruit shown in the succeeding verses, we will see just how powerful is this simple guidebook to the stormy voyages of human relationships.

Commentators and translators differ over the precise nature and shape of the opening premise. Is this about someone sinning in general, or sinning against someone, and is Jesus talking about sin within the church, or within a family? While the jury discusses their answer, we'll opt for the strongest evidence available, that Jesus is still addressing his disciples (see 18:1), having talked to them earlier in the discourse about the dynamics and values of his new kingdom community. They have been grappling with those still fundamental issues in any organisation: who is greatest and who has value?

Turning to the message itself, we see that Jesus presumes disagreement. Perhaps we can see it not so much a case of if, but when. It was true of his disciples and it is true of us today. We will sin against one another. We are imperfectly capable of doing and saying the most hurtful, spiteful things to our brothers and sisters, even those we are "united" with in Christ. Aside from the "sins of commission", my experience is we are more often guilty of the "sins of omission". We see a need and we ignore it; we could help and we turn a blind eye. Jesus tells us how to deal with such sins and I would suggest to you from the outset that his purpose is *unity*. His goal is a community of his people who know how to stick together.

Firstly, he says, when someone sins against you, you must go to him, privately. Confront the sinner with their offence.[103] There are few things more important, yet more awkward, in building relationships. Now there are a whole load of exceptional caveats to this rule, but before we hide behind those in hearing this teaching, let's see the genius of this life skill. Let it challenge you.

Let's imagine a scenario: you are having a harder-than-average week. Workload and pressure abounds and encouragements are few and far between. It seems your family and colleagues are wrapped up in their own worlds and too absorbed to notice you struggling. I know you've felt like that before. You're carrying a heavy load, literally, and you see a friend who you'd expect to notice that you need a hand, coming towards you empty handed.

They smile sweetly, showing superficial interest and ask that polite question, "Hello, how are you?"

"At last," you think, "someone cares!"

You warm to the opportunity and begin to open up to them, telling them your personal woes, grateful for their show of concern, and hoping they will notice your need of physical help, too. You're waiting to hear them offer to hold some of your burden, but instead their hand is in their pocket, pulling out their phone.

Now they're answering a text. You're there, talking, sharing, in need of compassion and help, physical assistance, and they aren't even listening. In fact, within just a moment they end the encounter:

"Anyway," they say, "Have a great week!" And they walk off.

It is one of the most common sins in church and the most endemic sins of humanity: the conscious unwillingness to offer help and show compassion. As a recipient on this occasion you are deeply hurt and adding that hurt to the burdens already carried.

However strongly you relate to this particular scenario, you can see that there are choices to be made as a result of everyday encounters. This teaching does not just apply with the big things, like when someone is a tragic victim of murder, rape, or racial abuse. Jesus' teaching should be applied to everyday disagreements because how we respond to this determines the strength of our community. Here is the weakest link in the chain of our unity.

Back to our scenario. What do you do? De-friend that person on Facebook? Send an abusive Tweet? More likely, you'll mention the event to someone else, maybe just in passing… "You'll never guess what. I bumped into so-and-so today and they could see I needed some help, with stress and frustration written all over my face, and even while I was talking to them (in response to their question!) they walked off! Incredible! Some people are so self-absorbed! The last thing I need is another person pretending to care!"

Jesus stands up in the classroom of discipleship, stops the recording and winds it back. Not to the point of the offence, but to the moment of the response. He recognises the sin committed, but wants to talk about your response. He says, "Confront them. Tell them they hurt you!"

Putting this into practice takes guts. In fact, it takes discipline and produces maturity. Following Jesus has always done that and living life his way is rarely comfortable. The genius of this one-to-one confrontation is that only you, the other party and God are aware of the incident. Let's say you go to the ignorant, uncaring offender and speak to them, in private, with the audience of One:

"You know when I saw you earlier, are you aware that you completely ignored me? I could have done with some help and your hands were free, but you didn't help. You could have offered to pray for me then and there, or at least waited until I finished saying what was going on, before you answered your phone!"

In this simplistic scenario, we can imagine the friend honestly seeing the error of their ways, apologising for being so ignorant and perhaps explaining that they were waiting for a text from the hospital because their elderly grandmother had recently had a stroke. Oh.

End of dispute. If anything, confrontation of this sort does more than remove the sting of a potentially poisonous division in the community. It actually makes it stronger.

Jesus says, this is how it should be among you. In my kingdom, people learn the art of disagreement and bring sins and failures, disputes and offences, into the light where they can handled with integrity. Now the next bullet-point in this presentation is what to do if that initial confrontation fails. For sure, that is sometimes the case. There is no repentance and no repair.

Our Lord teaches us that if at first we don't succeed in repairing the relationship, we should try again: *"Take one or two others with you and go back again, so that everything you say may be confirmed by two or three witnesses."*[104] Founded on the ancient Deuteronomic principle of requiring multiple witnesses to any crime,[105] Jesus urges us to choose dependable witnesses to this attempt at repair and reconciliation. Notice how the onus is on the offended, not the offender. This is radical teaching! We are here shown an example of making *every effort* to maintain unity within the body of believers. Again, if this approach is successful, if the wrongdoer repents and the relationship is restored, at most only five people, and one God, are aware of the nature of the dispute. The rest of the community, and the online world, can carry on regardless and there is little room for gossip, embellishment or exaggeration of the problem. We know how "Chinese Whispers" can work and we know how someone else's minor disagreement can become the dispute of the decade when the story is passed on. We don't live in a soap opera, but we know their scripts are inspired by our real, yet sad, propensity to make a meal of others' mistakes, feast on others' dysfunction and savour other people's broken lives for dessert. Jesus' protects us all from this tendency and says, if you have a disagreement, settle it, directly, and with the smallest audience possible. Heaven applauds when we do (we'll come to that in a bit).

If, and it is only an if, this attempt at small-group refereed arbitration fails, we must do something brave and something important: We must present the case to the church; to the *ekklesia*, interestingly, one of very few uses of this word in the gospels. Jesus has in mind all along, the moral and structural integrity of the church, the defined group of believers who are sharing in common life, love and purpose. He knows, as do we, that one small dispute can become cancerous in the body of Christ.

Jesus says in this unresolved case, if it comes to a head, let the church decide. Let the organisation (organism, actually) most at stake decide if this person has been wrongly judged or is wrongly unrepentant. If they are adjudged to be rebelling against the fellowship of believers, kick them out. I know commentators have squirmed at this suggestion, that Jesus is actually giving permission for people to be excluded from his body of believers. Those who see in their minds a pasty-skinned, moisturised, lamb-hugging Jesus, meek and mild, struggle to hear Jesus introducing a code of conduct that leaves people excluded.

Conversely, I see a Jesus who knows there are some wolves in sheep's clothing,[106] some unyielding, unrepentant, trouble-making busybodies who are not welcome in the kingdom of God.

Helen, my wonder-wife and closest, truest friend, was nearly taken away from me by cancer. In fact, for months a lump of tissue was growing in her leg that we had been told was a "fatty lump" worthy of (at some point) convenient removal at a later date. If it wasn't for the timely advice of one of our spiritual fathers, Tony Morton, and the intervention of Helen's parents and a private hospital, who knows how far this cancer would have spread? It was a tremendous shock to the consultant to find, when attempting the excision of some fatty tissue, a raging malignant secondary cancer.[107] As Tony Morton had said, a lump you're not sure about is "better out than in". It is like that in the church, you know. We are so weak in this regard, whilst Jesus was so strong. Paul's final instructions to the church in Rome follow up this teaching along the same lines:

"And now I make one more appeal, my dear brothers and sisters. Watch out for people who cause divisions and upset people's faith by teaching things contrary to what you have been taught. Stay away from them."[108]

This is not just a warning about doctrine, it also echoes a concern for those who divide instead of unite. Have nothing to do with such people and be willing to exclude them from your fellowship.

Are we getting the point here? I trust so. The clarity of Jesus' teaching in Matthew 18 reaches a crescendo of the kind of promises we love to take out of context and claim as if they are magic. Or, at least when only five people turn up for a church-wide prayer gathering:

"I tell you the truth, whatever you forbid on earth will be forbidden in heaven, and whatever you permit on earth will be permitted in heaven. I also tell you this: If two of you agree here on earth concerning anything you ask, my Father in heaven will do it for you. For where two or three gather together as my followers, I am there among them."[109]

At the risk of sounding simplistic, can we deduce from this some in-built conditions to answered prayer and the blessing of God's manifest presence when we gather as believers? I think we can, with integrity, extrapolate that this passage should be read as one holistic teaching. I would go so far as to assert that we have no right under heaven to expect to exercise significant spiritual authority (like binding and loosing in the heavenly realm), receive positive answers to "anything we ask" or experience the fullness of God's presence among us, if we refuse to maintain our unity; if we let the malignant tumours keep growing in the body. We sadly know what happens when diseases go untreated, when cancers run riot through the human body: self-destruction, secondary illness, physiological chaos and untimely death.

On that cheery note we should bring together these thoughts to recognise the importance of mastering the art of disagreement. I hope you can see just how applicable Jesus' teaching is in your own life, in your marriage, in your leadership team and in your church. We will unpack this in more detail in the next few chapters.

It takes a mature believer to confront division and arrest it before it spreads. It takes a Christ-like believer to stand up to the enemy's divisive schemes and send him packing, with resolve that the integrity of the church will not be diminished on their watch, through their embittered heart. It will take you and I freshly accepting this biblical challenge, becoming hard to offend and quick to forgive, to maintain the unity of the Spirit.

And we must. There is so much to this approach to life and godly community that we could linger here longer. We could reflect, furthermore, on Sacks' invitation to engage in fuller conversation and we could explore the intricacies and complexities of psychological makeup and how this formulaic approach sounds to the introvert and the chronically insecure. I encourage you to wrestle with these questions further. Suffice to highlight for now the central point: we are never going to build true Christian community, nor see the kingdom of God extended in our day, in our time, if we refuse to learn how to get on. And we will never get on if we refuse to disagree with integrity and find a way through into the harmony the world is longing to hear.

Endnotes
100. Ortberg, J, *Everybody's Normal Till You Get to Know Them*, 2003, 25
101. It is worth reading Francis Spufford's provocative book, *Unapologetic* (Faber & Faber, 2013) for a stronger, lucid explanation of what we have always known as sin.
102. Matthew 18:15-17
103. I was intrigued and amused to see Jonathan Sacks attributing such a concept (the willing confrontation of a perpetrator) to the Jewish mystic Maimonides, writing some 1200 years later! Jesus taught this first, okay? It is wisdom from heaven and the Great Rabbi Jesus has made this way clear. Thanks be to God.
104. Matthew 18:16
105. Deuteronomy 19:15, for example
106. Such are the false prophets, cf. Matthew 7:15
107. It is another whole story how Helen was healed. Following some powerful, anointed prayer after her diagnosis, and a God-given assurance the cancer had left, no further trace was found of any malignancy. It is a story of God's limitless power and we are grateful for his favour to preserve our lives to this day.
108. Romans 16:17
109. Matthew 18:18-20

11
The Power of Unity at Home

*"When you make the sacrifice in marriage, you're sacrificing not
to each other but to unity in a relationship."*
–Joseph Campbell

As we turn now to evermore practical applications of what we're
learning, we arrive at the kitchen tables, lounges, bedrooms and
under-stairs cupboards of our often messy, dysfunctional homes.
The rubber begins to hit the road right here, probably more
acutely than anywhere else.

Masterfully, the apostle Paul brings his magnificent "big-picture"
teaching of Christ's glorious, vibrant Church – on show as his
Masterpiece before all of creation – into focus in the home. Between
a husband and wife, between parents and their kids. Ephesians is
stunning in its scope and if we are to live life to the power of one we
will need to see things change in our closest relationships.

Even as I begin to write about such subjects I feel the egg-shells
beneath my toes. This is delicate ground and requires someone
more gifted and careful than I to walk forward without causing

undue pain. Nevertheless, we must look at what unity looks like in the home, and as we do so my prayer is that you will find it easy (if not comfortable) to apply this to your own specific situation.

What I do know is that behind the shiny front door of many church leaders, those who admonish us to be forgiving and encourage us to maturity, is a storm of unresolved conflict and damaging disappointment. We have seen up-close just how devastating it is when the courage to resolve issues and talk through pain and express stress, and genuinely listen to the other's point of view, is lost altogether. I mention church leaders because I am one and also because we do well to highlight the potential for a gap to grow between what we believe and teach and what we do. It is a form of cognitive dissonance, where we become convinced that our situation is unique: "You haven't tried to be married to my husband, he's impossible!" So we slowly close the door on trying.

We are called to make *every effort* to maintain the unity of the Spirit and I believe this urging should and does apply to Christian marriage. It is the first field of play, the primary area of responsibility, for many of us. Do we give up, or do we persevere? Please understand, I am not a marriage counsellor, nor am I the person to advise you on the pastoral theology that applies to every form of engagement, mixed-race marriage, divorce, second marriage, and so on. My desire here is to inspire and encourage you, in whichever situation you find yourself, to consider afresh how you can cooperate with God and enjoy more fully the unity of the Spirit.

It's not good enough, in my humble opinion, to have subjects in a home that "we just don't talk about any more". Where is the unity in a home when certain topics are off-limits and communication is stilted and disjointed? Awkward conversations and long silences keep relationships in the shallows, failing to find depth for fear of saying the wrong thing. This is a call to push through some of those pain-barriers and find a deeper way.

I happen to be married to one of the most communicative people I know. It is (honestly) one of Helen's many great qualities. She seems to always have a perspective to share, a question to ask, something to say. It's not gossip and it isn't trivia. She is a deep thinker, an eager learner, and a practical strategist. With a remarkable ability to juggle a number of trains of thought (if you can juggle trains; sounds heavy!), she is great fun to have conversation with. It is just as well, because I love to talk, too. In our best moments as husband and wife, and in co-leadership of the church we serve, the conversation is flowing freely and there is due attention given to what's important, with a healthy mix of banter thrown in.

Interrupt this flow for any length of time (like for a three-month sabbatical to write this book) and we are headed for trouble. We enjoyed hours of uninterrupted conversation on our four thousand mile roadtrip across the USA in 2014 (we did stop to get petrol!). It was amazing, relaxed, and did wonders for our sense of togetherness as a couple, and when the free and unhindered discussion is flowing, I have noticed how it sets our whole family up for more laughter and a greater sense of unity.

Truth is, we need to talk.

In fact, we need to argue, listen, disagree, forgive, dream, reason, take time out, and then come together with new thoughts to make our marriage work. We have, by God's grace, been married for twenty years and we are still discovering changing parts of ourselves and each other that need talking through and figuring out. We have decided that silence between us is not our default mode.

There was a time when I was in a particular grump and feeling less than cheerful towards Helen. Hard to imagine, I know. Let's just say it was a bad day. I did something for the first time: I turned off the tap of affirmation that typically runs freely from my lips. This particular gift of mine veers close to insincerity, but is a habit I consciously hold onto every day: I tell Helen I love her throughout the day and affirm who she is to me, how glad I am she's mine and all that other gushy stuff that would make you cringe. If I'm honest, 99% of the time I really mean what I am saying. Or 95% perhaps! I grew up in a home where my loving, affirming parents would cheer anything I did that was even vaguely applaudable and I guess I have picked up this tendency towards effusive affection. On most days this is a desirable and positive quality. On this particular day, I was feeling so fed up I stopped saying these loving words. The well of vocal affirmation was dry. Would Helen notice, I wondered? Oh yes, she noticed! She hated not hearing how I felt. After we talked through the dispute (and we did), normal service resumed, quite rightly.

It seems to me that silence in a marriage is the convenient way to a form of peace that isn't really the kind of unity the Spirit longs for us to enjoy. In our marriages do we actually celebrate our differences? Do you delight in how different your husband is from you? Do you recognise the diversity within your home and actually celebrate just how differently you see, feel, think and work? Helen and I are still learning this one. She is writing on this subject, namely the danger of engaging in "friendly fire" between the sexes. It is a challenge to couples to stop competing against each other, recognising that our enemy is not our spouse. We have a common enemy and his plan is to destroy and divide. One of his favourite targets is the covenantal commitment between man and wife.

Paul writes, in his application of unity to marriage, *"submit to one another out of reverence for Christ."*[110] It is the foundation of his teaching on unity in the home: mutual submission. He goes on to apply this to the distinct and unique roles of the husband and wife, exchanging respect and love, sacrifice and cleansing, as a beautiful parallel of how Christ relates to his Church. Stunning teaching. Suffice to highlight here that the hallmarks of a marriage made in heaven are the same we have been discussing in a wider field: diversity, harmony, humility, dignity, generosity, maturity. In God's grand design our homes should be free from pride and superiority, fear and inferiority, ambiguity regarding commitment and uniformity regarding personality and perspective. You see, the unity of Spirit must be maintained in the home.

When we apply this to parenting (and Paul does this, too[111]) and how children relate to their mum and dad, we note that Paul is affording children their dignity, too. A powerful new approach in the first century. As Nick Page explains,

"Christian communities were different. The Didache contains an injunction against abortion and infanticide. In fact, Christians would go round rescuing whatever children they could."[112]

One thing we should consider seriously when it comes to a distinctively Christian value of children: we should let them be themselves. Not in some hands-off, go-to-bed-when-you-want absenteeism, but I mean in terms of expecting them to be gloriously unique. We have some dear friends in Derry/Londonderry, Northern Ireland, and they have four wonderful kids. Brian and Judith are a fantastic couple leading a great church,

Cornerstone City Church (more on that in due course). They spring to mind because their four kids were born within a matter of minutes. Yes, they are the proud owners (?!) of quadruplets and on my first visit to their home I was so warmly greeted by all four of them, 9 years old at the time. I was amazed to see just how wonderfully, beautiful unique they all are, in personality, in their smile, in the way they talked and the things they were into. It's a simple parable of diversity that can inform our families, too. They have the same parents, share the same bedroom in the same home and receive from their folks the same unconditional love and affection, and yet they will grow up to be uniquely crafted individuals with their own destinies in God. Isn't that amazing and shouldn't we celebrate their differences?

I am sure (if you have kids) you see characteristics you like in all your children. After all, they got something from you, didn't they?! There are probably some qualities you prefer, or resonate with more than others, and without doubt there will be qualities, not-so-qualities, idiosyncrasies and habits that have the potential to drive you crazy. We would do well to heed Paul's advice and not exasperate our kids,[113] but rather cooperate with God and see their vibrant uniqueness woven into the rich tapestry of our family, as a gift to the wider world.

Marriage, and I believe other relationships in the home too,[114] are meant to be an illustration of, an example of and witness to, the unity of the Godhead and the unity of Christ with his Church. The mysterious unity we have been exploring all along is to be found in the Christian home, in the covenant of Christian marriage and in the dignified rearing of children.

My hypothesis in this final section of the book is simplistic, but I still believe it. Let me explain: with the melody and words of Psalm 133's promise providing the background music, we should be able to cooperate with God's unifying work in different spheres and expect blessing in those spheres. So, if a husband and wife are dwelling together in unity, the family is blessed. As we will see, if the leaders in a team or a church are truly united, the corresponding team, organisation or church will be blessed. What's more, if churches are united across a town or community, then the community will be blessed. We all want that aim.

So, isn't it time we put some fresh effort to maintain unity in our marriages in our homes? How? That's for you to wrestle through and I know that wrestling will involve some healthy arguments, resolved disagreements and a lot of genuine listening. But God's grace is sufficient.

As the saying goes, charity (generous love) begins at home and so does unity. Let's start from here and move onwards and outwards, in the power of the Spirit.

Endnotes
110. Ephesians 5:21
111. See Ephesians 6:1-4
112. Page, Nick, 2012, 102
113. Ibid.
114. See Ephesians 5:32

12
The Power of Unity in Your Team

"Coming together is a beginning, and staying together is progress,
but only when teams sweat together
do they find success."
–John Maxwell

Some of my fondest memories in life involve that intoxicating mix of physical effort, personal challenge, costly sacrifice, coordinated actions and against-the-odds victory. Basically, I mean winning with a team.

I would like to pretend that I played rugby (Union) at a high level, but I am not sure the English-Inter-Bible-College-League (made up name) is what you would call "high level"! You wouldn't even call it "low level". It's just a mixed-age bunch of theology students grunting in a poorly-drained field instead of reading Karl Barth. Nevertheless, I and my team-mates will never forget the afternoon we drove over to Croydon to play our arch-rivals, Spurgeons, and beat them on their own turf. Their own mud, I mean. It was the most wonderful feeling, the topic of exaggerated reminiscence ever since (including my recollections now)! As I recall that afternoon I can feel that glow of team success. From the front row to the fullback, we put all our effort into the common cause and the result of our unity and effort that day was a glorious victory, jovial back-slapping, and a sense of supremacy against a rival. If we could bottle that feeling and harness that power in all the teams we serve in, more would be achieved and more people would enjoy the achievement. In the light of this, what is the power of unity in a team?

If you are a keen reader on leadership, or have received teambuilding coaching at work, you will recognise here only a superficial treatment of a massive subject. My intention here is to thread in what we have been looking at thus far: the Spirit of unity and the refreshing blessing it brings, and see how it might work out in a team context.

Firstly, the need for healthy disagreement and open dialogue: it is hard to overstate the importance of honest, open conversation in building a healthy team. We have experienced mixed success over the years in teambuilding, not least in seeking to identify, gather, inspire, lead and equip the leadership team of our church. If you are a team leader, you know that the relational and functional unity we all dream of is very hard to achieve, but pursue it, we must.

Teambuilding is agonising at times, like the fifteenth attempt at a lineout in rugby when the hooker still can't throw a ball straight. How hard it is to throw the flippin' ball straight?! But when I'm a prop (and not the hooker) and it is his job to throw it in, I can't do it for him. I have to stand, grunt, hope, wait, moan. Wait for the ball. Then stand, grunt, wait... you get the idea. A healthy team carries the qualities of rich diversity where we need the other players on the team to perform, to do their bit.

The Spirit of unity urges us and (graciously) enables us to lean on the gifts and strengths, and roles of others. If teammates are having a bad day, they may need someone else to sub in. More likely though, they need some encouragement to keep going, to not give up, to try again. You see, the point at which a team dynamic can change is often the moment when communication goes up a level. Silence leads to demoralisation and then defeat.

We looked earlier at the anatomy of Christian unity, inspired by the Triune harmony of the Godhead, and at the prospect of joining in with that symphony of mutual respect and love here on the earth. The new kingdom is one vast team of teams, an orchestra of orchestras, with Christ as the Head and Lord, the Author and conductor of our faith. The teams we serve on and lead, can and should sympathetically vibrate to the melodies of heaven. We can build teams with dignity for every member of the team, where generosity of spirit sets an atmosphere of affirmation, a celebration of how different each part of the team is. Whilst there should be consistency of character and virtue, there will also be freedom from predictability and uniformity.

Reflecting back on the last couple of decades, I can recognise some serious mistakes I have made as a Christian leader. Perhaps these have been accentuated because of my youth and inexperience, but I cannot hold that up as an excuse. The reasons for most of these failures is my own insecurity, a fear of failing and (without doubt) an anxiety about confronting people with their failings and our differences. See, there you have it, a fear of recognising differences, and relational dysfunctions, and dealing with them at first sight. It is better to nip issues in the bud than let them fester. If you look around a room at a team you genuinely don't have confidence in, sooner or later something is going to need to change. Either the membership of the team will need to change, or the atmosphere and the approach to leading it.

The power of unity in a team is so potent, holds such potential, and the effects of victory so far reaching. As we have seen, the fuel of this unity is a spirit of generous acceptance of other members, matched by an absolute determination to talk things through and really listen. I do regret times when I was passively dishonest about my confidence in a team member. I should have taken them aside and simply said, "Sorry, I am just not sure we can be on the same team. This isn't working is it?" and seen what would have come of the ensuing dialogue. Instead I just thought it and suffered the consequences. The other party had no right to reply because we didn't have the conversation. Not only that, in the name of some form of apparent "agreement" I was actually masking a foundational disunity in the team. It is like wallpapering over the cracks in a wall while a house's subsidence continues unabated. Don't make that mistake. The call to Christian maturity calls us to learn the art of humble disagreement with a view to building a unity that is real.

We have had many people over the years join and then leave our church family. I have written elsewhere about what we have learned from this. Church leaders will know the agony of people who say they will cover your back becoming the ones who stab you themselves. Ouch. I don't want to exaggerate the point, but I wish some of these believers over the years would have sat us down and told us exactly what was the problem they had with us; why they couldn't follow our lead, why they couldn't serve on our team. But then again I am pretty sure many would say, "Tim, we would have told you had you asked," or, "we are not sure you would handle the criticism with dignity. There was no safe place within which to share what we really felt." They may well be right, and if you are one of those people who were hurt in this way, Helen and I are truly sorry for any pain arising from our inexperience and our insecurity.

So many mistakes to learn from. I hope and trust now we are growing in our ability to build and galvanise a team. In Wellspring Church we seem to be getting better at honest, open dialogue at a Senior Leadership Team and staff team level. For sure, we all value the unity we have discovered and we want to see it deepen. A team enjoying a deep sense of unity to a common cause, with generous self-sacrifice and Christ-like, confident humility abounding, has enormous potential to bless our world. This book is a call to enjoy unity, to enjoy the experience of comradery and the sweetness of shared victories, knowing that a prize awaits all those who pursue it.

13
The Power of Unity in Your Church

"One hundred religious persons knit into a unity by careful organisations do not constitute a church any more than eleven dead men make a football team.
The first requisite is life, always."
–A W Tozer

That summer was a defining season in my life. So disturbing and disappointing was it that I am not sure I have recovered. Maybe I never will. It was the year our church fell apart, split down the middle. I was fifteen and joyfully part of one of the most dynamic, powerful local churches in the country. The hallmarks of Norwich Christian Fellowship at that time were supernatural faith, great Bible teaching, dynamic worship and the best youth group ever. Many of the young people went to the church's own school in the city, but my brother and I, the rural outsiders, were warmly included in camping trips in Sherwood Forest, night hikes, and full-on musical productions. I can honestly say I haven't heard of a more dynamic, Spirit-filled, fun youth group.

So many rich memories, so much togetherness and (amongst the youth at least), such unity. Then came the news. The Elders had come to a point of fundamental disagreement about the direction of the fellowship and members were being asked which leader they trusted enough to follow.

It was devastating to see and experience the fallout from this division. Even as I recall it, something moves me deep within because a family was torn apart that summer, because the leaders couldn't get it together. Inevitably, relationships between our families became stretched, loyalties threatened and out of one united family came two battered groups of followers and then a whole load who have not been part of a church since. Because of this experience I have been able to offer some (limited) empathy to children whose parents have divorced. I think I know how that can feel. To this day I still reckon there was another way that this division was avoidable. It wasn't about one leader's unrepentant moral failure, nor another elder's conscious rebellion to Jesus' teaching. Our whole church split because of a leadership struggle and (dare I suggest) because of a failure to find the higher way of humility, generosity and the building of God's kingdom instead of man's empire.

Those closest to the centre of that particular division, the men and women wiser at the time than adolescent me, living miles away from the disagreements, may explain to me how it really was. I have got some of the details wrong. But I saw the devastation and I felt the pain. I lost friends and I have grieved over those who gave up on the Church because of that church split. Hear the ancient cry of heaven: *that we might be one.*

There is another season that brings tears to my eyes for altogether different reasons. These memories crystallise when I think about the opening day of The Wellspring Church Centre, our purpose-built home in the heart of Watford. It is a long story, a story that started in 2003 with a prophecy from our dear friend Peter Stott who foresaw something we weren't even looking for: a church building. On the opening day, 19th March 2011, Peter and his wife Mariette stood in our newly completed, £1.7million building, alongside the builders, architects, other church leaders, Elected Mayor Dorothy Thornhill and our whole congregation to celebrate what God had done. Even now I marvel at the achievement, because though I had a front-row seat to the planning and fund-raising, the vision-casting and praying, I cannot account for how it all came together except one thing: *unity.*

Many marvelled at how smoothly, how effortlessly, the staff and leadership team made the Official Opening Day happen. It was a remarkable event, with 300 people moving around the building, offering hospitality, welcoming guests, performing in the band and so on. However, the day itself was just an expression of where we had arrived as a church. We were unified, united in our mission and sharing common values as we were determined to see our common vision become a reality. From the sketchy plans came a beautifully finished building. To get there, the diverse gifts of many had been employed and everyone's gift mattered. I remember a young lad bringing his money jar to one of our gift days to contribute to the £1.4million builder's contract.

I think that was the same week we had our biggest single gift given, £30,000, and both were as significant. In fact, somehow a church family of around 80 households saw around £600,000 raised (in addition to a property sale, mortgage and some government grants) to see The Wellspring doors open. Incredible.

The power of unity in a local church is transformational. It leaves a legacy of hope in communities, brings joy to its members and I believe it brings great joy to God. Our story with The Wellspring is just an example, but I can honestly say that there was a smile in heaven on that opening day when we played Peter Stott's prophecy on the screen (set to music, of course, with photos of our journey thus far). In the supportive presence of our Mayor, we laughed and cried at the 8-year-old oracle describing a glass-fronted building erected on land given by local authorities, as a source and place of refreshing for the community. The power of unity.

Let's get down to some daily nitty-gritty, though. This unity is not available in a book and it isn't downloadable to your phone. It can't be sent by email, though a badly worded email could damage it! Greater, wiser leaders than me have written more helpfully on this subject than I am able, but in our pursuit of God's best for our communities we must explore further what harmony sounds like in our churches. And I don't mean on Sundays ... necessarily. There are some keys to building a church of unity and we will take a few moments to imagine how the Spirit of unity wants to work in your church family.

Honest leaders

Much is written and asserted about the primary, crucial and pivotal role of leadership in a local church. We saw it in Ephesians 4 and we know it from experience, too. Whatever our ecclesiology, our doctrine and structure of church governance, we know for sure that leaders can split churches, ruin churches, encourage churches, neglect churches. Often literally, a local church's leaders hold the key to the building of a fruitful local church. My contribution to this part of the discussion is quite simple, really. I think the Spirit of unity is calling church leaders to honesty. Honesty about who they are and who they're not. Honesty within teams and honesty even, to the whole congregation. By my reckoning, some of that honesty needs to be about job descriptions and church members' expectations. Too many leaders are pretending to be someone they are not, trying to fulfil a role and meet expectations they can't actually fulfil. Perhaps you know what I mean? If you're not gifted by God as a preacher, stop comparing yourself to the greatest communicators alive in the Church today, it's not your calling. Maybe you're a loving pastor, excellent with children, or a patient, insightful counsellor. Be who you are and be honest about who you're not.

Honesty with congregations falls in line with this. People can discern more than they let on about the strengths and weaknesses of their leaders. They'll discuss them over Sunday lunch, but not very often with you. Why? Because they (mostly) don't want you to leave them. They do want you to play to your strengths though and let others bring their strengths alongside your weaknesses. The destination is team-wide unity, harmonised gifts, diversity working together and (as we have clearly established so far), the key is honest conversation.

Helen and I are on a journey with this (as with it all). Having seen church leaders fail and churches split, you'll understand why I have remained determined to be accountable and open to criticism. I'm afraid of my own potential for megalomania. To this end, we keep trying different methods and approaches for annual reviews, Helen and I (for a vulnerable moment) becoming the subject of discussion regarding strengths and "areas for growth". The majority of such reviews are uncomfortable (do you love your annual appraisal at work?) and some have been set up wrong so that their fruit is harder to see. But the more we work things through, the closer we are getting (I trust) to having the right people in the room, with the right goal in mind, to help us grow as leaders. And all along what we are seeking to set up is an honest conversation.

Whatever your church context, may I suggest that your leadership members, and the team as a whole (whatever shape that takes), could benefit from some more open, honest conversations? Sparks will fly, egos will be dented and foundations will be questioned. Maturing leaders will take the time to respond and not react, to listen and not bite back. Take note: lasting unity is stunted by superficiality, but it thrives in the soil of honesty.

Faithful followers

The story of Jonathan and his armour-bearer is intriguing and inspiring. If you haven't read it, take a look at 1 Samuel 14. It is rightly used as a powerful example of the difference made by faithful "follow-ship". Jonathan one day decides to leave the Israelite camp, the vast army following his father the king, to take on their Philistine enemy. Instead of waiting for the enemy to attack them as they rested under the shade of a pomegranate tree (sounds nice, doesn't it), Jonathan has a moment of "perhaps..".

"'Let's go across to the outpost of those pagans,' Jonathan said to his armour bearer. 'Perhaps the Lord will help us, for nothing can hinder the Lord. He can win a battle whether he has many warriors or only a few!' 'Do what you think is best,' the armour bearer replied. 'I'm with you completely, whatever you decide.'"[115]

I have heard and read some inspiring sermons on this passage and even preached it myself. It is a great story. The Lord confirms his agreement with Jonathan's "perhaps" and blesses his follower's faithfulness, and these two men rout the enemy. Chaos ensues in the Philistine camp and then heaven responds with a devastating earthquake. Saul and the many look on, amazed. The central idea we glean from this is that there is great power in the unity confirmed by great followers, not just great leaders.

In your local church, how many people actually trust the leaders? How many have the grace, faith and determination to say this to their leaders: "Do what you think is best. I'm with you completely, whatever you decide."

The Spirit of unity is looking to move in and through your local church. He wants to confirm old things and do some new things. He wants to defeat your enemies and build the Father's kingdom in your community. A united kingdom. To achieve this, he has given you leaders who have within their hearts a dream, a hope, an idea, a "perhaps" or two, and the Spirit of God is looking to inspire you, and people like you, to be faithful followers. Not passive critics. Not onlookers sitting in the shade, but armour-bearers willing to risk it all.

Whether by many or by few, the Spirit of God can do a lot when leaders and followers are united in a common, kingdom cause.

Common Vision

This seems almost too obvious to mention, but if the leaders and members of a local church can't see the same thing (even vaguely) they are not united. Without vision, all constraint and limitation on possible activity is lifted off and the people run wild.[116] Vision channels our efforts, focuses our prayers and unites our contributions.

Returning to the earlier image of a hand-woven rug of great

beauty, we recognise the need to see a bigger picture, a finished picture, before putting finger to thread. What good is a box of jigsaw pieces without the image on the box? Helen Keller said, *"The only thing worse than being blind is having sight but no vision."* Sadly, too many churches have lost sight of the invisible. Leaders have given up on God-given dreams, often because of the failure to openly cast it with conviction to the teams and people around them. Very often the vision is lost because no one carries it except the leaders. Followers expect words to become actions without their personal contribution.

Much has been written and taught about this. Leaders like Bill Hybels and Andy Stanley have repeatedly and powerfully asserted the need for churches (and organisations, businesses and so on) to fully embrace the risky, bigger-than-us visions God gives. In your church there is great power in the united pursuit of a common vision, be it a brick-building project or a people-building project, a mission-sending project or a vison to change lives in your community. Lost sight of it? Rub your eyes and ask God to show you again.

Shared Values

"There's a time to cast vision, and then there's a time to instil viable value." – Bill Hybels

It has often been said that in a collective of people, whether a family or church, business or corporation, even a town or a city, "culture always wins". This refers to the values that undergird that grouping, whether those values are spoken or unspoken, consciously reinforced and repeated, or never referenced. Your church has values, so does mine. What are they?

Perhaps the values of your church are a willingness to serve, a trust of leaders and a generosity towards others: you never feel awkward about an offering, or being asked to go on the welcome rota, nor does anyone wince (or fall asleep) when the leadership share the way forward. How would you know if these were the values in your operation? Look around. You'll know. It will be obvious. If you look around and you see cynicism and disconnection, mistrust and tight-fistedness pretty much across the board, you know there is a disconnect.

It doesn't matter what you *think* your values are as a church – as our friend Joel Holm pointed out to us on a visit to Watford one time, people don't recite your values statement before they head for bed each night. Values statements are helpful (and we are in a process of restating ours in Wellspring Church) but what actually comes into play in a church is the values people *hold*.

The sweet-spot in a team, and in a church, is when people have seen a common vision and then live, and talk, and pray, and give, and work not just with a common vision, but with shared values, too. As John Maxwell says,

"Values hold the team together, provide stability for the team to grow upon, measure the team's performance, give direction and guidance and attract like-minded people."

So too in a church and it doesn't take much imagination to see the community-changing potential in your local fellowship, and mine, of a diverse group of people, living in humility enjoying open conversation, celebrating their differences but living by shared values. Here the Lord commands a blessing.

We can see ahead, and glimpse beyond our lifetimes even, our ultimate vision: heaven's harmonious unity around the throne of God, where every tribe and tongue worships the God of Abraham. Within our lifetimes, in our churches today, can we also see the urgent and pressing need to do away with petty divisions and loosely held loyalties and keep the unity of the Spirit who has brought us together for his purpose? Unified church families, united leadership teams, fast-forgiving and generous communities of faith can and will produce much fruit. Don't stand in the way. Be part of the solution, not the problem.

In the next chapter we will turn our attention to the most challenging application I have come across, and one with the most potential to express the unity of the Spirit in our towns and cities, namely unity across the Church. So help us God.

Endnotes
115. 1 Samuel 14:6f
116. This is one paraphrase of Proverbs 29:18

14
The Power of Unity in Your Community

"Hope is where the door is
When the Church is where the war is..."
–U2

Though I was a young lad, I remember watching the documentary footage in absolute shock. They were playing news clips from the Bloody Sunday riots, the Bogside Massacre in Derry, Northern Ireland. Fourteen men and boys were gunned down by British Paras as a disproportionate response to a sectarian march. I don't even begin to comprehend all that happened, but what is patently clear is that this city is the epitome of a community divided. At least, it was.

Even now, whether I write Derry or Londonderry I am making a religio-political statement about whose city it really is. This is such a contentious issue, the signs on the city's roundabouts simply say, "Welcome to the Walled City". Dublin band U2's protest song about the woeful day that kick-started generational bitterness on a whole new scale, expresses a godly lament at this shameful disharmony:

"And the battle's just begun
There's many lost, but tell me who has won?
The trench is dug within our hearts
And mothers, children, brothers, sisters torn apart
Sunday, Bloody Sunday...
How long must we sing this song?
'cause tonight...we can be as one,
Tonight...tonight..."

The saddest part of this whole Irish division, the most shameful aspect to all the Troubles and the ancient disharmony in that land, is that the Christian faith (or at least religion that claims to follow Christ) is at the very heart of it all.

Catholic or Protestant? These faith positions and traditions have become inextricably linked with the factions dividing Ireland: Republican or Unionist; pro-Irish or pro-British. Quite literally, the city is divided down the middle (by the River Foyle) with one side Catholic and the other, Protestant. Whilst visiting the city recently I was driven by our friend Pastor Brian Somerville through Bogside (on the Western, Catholic Cityside) and was advised that holding a Union Jack out the window would invite a violent response. So I didn't.

The situation in The Walled City is the most vivid picture of a divided community I have come across and at the heart of the division is the very fellowship of faith, the very stewards of hope, that should unite a community under God: the Church.

However, and it is a tentatively glorious however, God has not given up on working in that city. Far from it. The city is beginning to come together, helped to some extent by the amnesty of guns and the dialogue of politicians. I believe through and beyond these things, that the Spirit of unity is at work. The physical manifestation of this move is The Peace Bridge, opened by an EU Commissioner flanked with leaders from both side of the Foyle's divide, in 2011. It is a foot and cycle bridge which joins the Waterside and Cityside communities and on that opening day our friends in Cornestone City Church were there in number, in full support of what this bridge represented. It is time for a generation to come together and move on from the pain of the past. What is needed? To let mercy triumph over judgment and to believe for a new community of grace in Christ, no longer shackled by the reciprocal violence of our forefathers. I was delighted to hear that the Somerville's church, full of the Spirit, were welcoming Catholics and Protestants into a special prayer tent on that opening day. 3,000 visited. Wonderful.

As Brian and I stood on that bridge in December 2014, talking about the power of a bridge to unite two sides of a divide, he told me of a day when the whole of Cornerstone joined hands from one end of The Peace Bridge to the other, praying for God's blessing on their city. Amongst their members, praying for the future of their one city were former Catholic paramilitaries whose family were killed in the Troubles, and former Protestants who had marched in support of the British Army. Instead of those denominational, divisive labels, they now simply call themselves "Christians". Church members, joined by American missionaries and then an increasing number of "random" members of the public, joined hands and prayed. This is an example to us all.

Ed Silvoso is an inspiring advocate for inter-church collaboration and for a prayerful, supernatural unity in cities. He sees this whole drama played out in the heavenly realms (in tune with Paul's assertions in Ephesians) and testifies:

"When Satan has the upper hand in a city, we always find a church that is deeply divided with members, congregations and denominations that are angry at each other."[117]

We have to stand in faith to believe that in cities like Derry, and where you live, the long-time rule of the devil of division is coming to an end.

As mentioned earlier, I have been a passionate and dedicated believer in inter-church unity since the day we started leading Wellspring Church. In fact, my experiences in Norwich and the efforts on the part of some key leaders to make special effort in this regard probably laid the foundations. I began then to understanding something of the equality under God of every congregation and the need to serve God together. I remain convinced as ever (hence I am writing this book) that it pleases the Lord when his people keep "low walls" between local churches in our community. This has not been just a divine download, it is an ongoing exploration. It is the result of the open-hearted and inspiring influence of fellow leaders in Watford over the years. Ministers like Graham Cracknell, Chris Cottee, John Aldis, Roy Young. Praying with them, dreaming with them, planning, and serving alongside them, has reinforced my convictions about this subject.

Christians Across Watford has a strapline which remains our experience and our goal: "Learning to be one Church in this town and for this town". We believe that in God's eyes, from his perspective, there is in actual fact only one Church in Watford. We have many congregations, different styles of worship, contrasting approaches to leadership and mission, but we are parts of a greater whole. We often say that if Jesus wrote a letter to us (as in Revelation), he'd write a letter, "To the Church in Watford". We have identified in Watford what this unity may involve, namely the importance and significance of uniting in *Prayer, Praise, Partnership* and *Proclamation*.

Applying all we have seen already on this journey, at least in principle, is simple. In your community and mine, diverse and different churches can and should humbly consider other churches for what they are. Not with an inferiority complex because another church is bigger, or has a shinier newsletter, nor arrogantly looking down on the more struggling congregations. Sober and honest conversation about who we are and what we're each about, gives room for God to bless our differences and unite us for a greater cause. In fact, no one church can reach and bring life to a given neighbourhood or community. For a start, there will be some people in your neighbourhood that love organs and hate guitars. Still others have never learned to pray in silence, while others need to be told what to pray; not because they're weaker, but because they're different. In this way, we must learn to celebrate difference. It is critical to our mission together that we learn to rejoice that other churches are distinctly unique, in contrast to our own, and not deficient because of this. In increasingly diverse communities, do we need an increasingly varied approach to reaching people and teaching them the ways of walking with Christ? I think so.

Remember Jesus' prayer:

"I pray that they will all be one, just as you and I are one—as you are in me, Father, and I am in you. And may they be in us so that the world will believe you sent me."[118]

The world is watching. While other religious groups terrorise and wreak havoc, threatened by difference and fractured by sectarian divides, it is time for the Church to (humbly) show a better way. Not to talk about unity, but to enjoy it and let the fruit emerge.

What is needed in our neighbourhoods is a genuine, lasting unity. Reliable leadership is required, where ministers are not fighting over position but instead recognising those who are gifted and called to lead forward the united Church. If this leadership recognises a common "kingdom" vision that includes and engages the wider Christian community, the potential for blessing on that town or city is enormous. We have begun to see some of this in Watford and the fruit has been fresh and various. In the last 15 years of praying, witnessing, praising, meeting, eating and serving together we have seen the Watford Town Centre Chaplaincy established. This is now mobilising over thirty volunteers in workplaces and public arenas, shops and civic centres as well as teams of Street Angels who serve the night-club community on the late-night streets of our town. We have a thriving Foodbank, Christian resource centre, a Christmas Hamper project, leadership training academy and ever-strengthening links with the YMCA and other service providers.

In 2015 we are leading the way in conducting a Faith Action Audit and planning further united outreach and prayer events. In fact, it seems impossible to sum it all up and I am inevitably going to leave something out, because what we have seen has a Spirit-inspired life of its own. No one except the God who unites us deserves any credit. We're just cooperating with him.

You may be reading this and wondering where this is going, how far do we go with this inter-church unity thing? Good question. For some, it is a painful experience even attending a Churches Together prayer meeting once a month. All that "My church is bigger than your church" insecure banter and the often-laboured decisions to not do very much. I know, you wouldn't lead it that way, and you wonder if it is worth it. You may ask, "What are we achieving?" and that is one question to be answered. But so is, "Who are we serving?", "Are we seeing the bigger picture?" and most importantly, "Can I see the work of the Spirit in the ministry of others?" Humility can show us that in other denominations, in churches so different from our own, in whispers and in loud praise, in African choruses and in Latin prayers, the Spirit is at work. He is the same Spirit who longs to draw God's children together (all those who can by his power call him, "Abba"), even where you live, for a higher purpose than you can see.

What we have seen taking place in Watford, this movement of Spirit-inspired unity, is happening in new ways all over the world. In the late 1990s many were inspired, as were we, by the testimony of people like Ed Silvoso, Ruth Ruibal, Peter Wagner and the producers of the Transformation videos. We were inspired to think again about our towns and cities, pulling focus on the kind of communities we could imagine them becoming and the kind of transformation we dreamed of witnessing in people's lives. This was about pastoring our communities, not just our churches.

Roger Sutton, Steve Clifford, Dave King, Ewen Huffman and many others have been working with the support of the EA, to encourage and facilitate the "Gather" Movement in the UK. Their aim is to add fuel to the fires already burning of country-wide inter-church collaboration, sharing faith, examples and wisdom. I believe the next generation will be very grateful for their pursuit of the unity of the Spirit in our land. Much fruit will come from this.

I do have some unanswered questions about how far this journey should take us. I have heard of an inter-denominational church-plant in Southampton, and wonder how that works. I wonder how effective inter-church prayer meetings can be and want to be free of a wrong sense of obligation to a particular "style". What's more, in leading a growing, vibrant church, with a big vision to bring community transformation, I wonder how a more apostolic-centre form of church relates to those operating with a more pastoral model.[119] The key question being, how do stronger church-planting churches stay truly united with the wider Christian community whilst still carrying out a God-given mandate to pioneer the new? These questions deserve greater treatment. I think part of the answer can be found in Gempf's "sympathetic vibrations" analogy. Perhaps it is a case of turning up the volume on whatever the Spirit is doing, through whomever, and allowing others to resonate and harmonise accordingly.

I explained in a previous chapter about my simple theory, namely that unity between a husband and wife brings blessing in their home (and conversely division causes damage). Additionally, as we looked at in chapter 12 and 13, a unified leadership team can bring a blessing on the church they serve. Expand that to a community and I believe we have the greatest potential for bringing change, spiritually and practically, through the unity of the Christian community, across traditions and divides. When your churches and charities unite and acknowledge the lordship of Christ in your community, declaring his name over and above the name of any one church or ministry, your village, town or city will be blessed. We hold some keys here, let's use them to unlock floodgates of healing and blessing on our streets. Can God bless division amongst his people? Not so sure. Can God do a lot when his people gather, pray and serve in unity? Oh yes.

This reminds me of that day (I think it was July, 2000) when we gathered for the first of many annual open-air services as Christians Across Watford. We stood and worshipped around a mobile stage on Cassibury Park, praying for the town before the Rainbow Festival. Newly elected Mayor Dorothy Thornhill tapped me on the shoulder before she led a prayer and asked if we could end the service by singing her favourite song. So we did, loudly, jubilantly: "Our God Reigns!"

I believe that day something broke over Watford in the places we cannot see, opening the way for God to do great things in our town. What has followed since around that town is quite remarkable. Watford is thriving in so many ways. The town has become a place of world-class filmmaking and corporate importance with key transportation links and some of the best State-funded schools in the country. Even new churches are being built on Council-owned land! There is so much more to be done, of course, but let's acknowledge God's blessing when we see it.

As we consider the power of unity in communities, we should give thanks to God for examples of his work underway in our day, in other parts of our nation. A prime example is Salford. Just a few years ago on the wasteland left by the docks in this once thriving but now impoverished corner of Greater Manchester, a pastor and a small group of believers prayed and prophesied life over the abandoned community. They began to pray and prophesy about Salford becoming a place of worldwide influence. It was heard from heaven that "The nations will come to Salford and Salford will go to the nations." It seemed impossible. The best victories do. A united group of church leaders and church members held onto that word and prayed and believed.

Now, on that same piece of land, the BBC has moved much of its television and radio base. From here the BBC News is broadcast live, so too the BBC World Service. Subsequently, many global broadcasters, filmmakers and television production companies have made their home on those abandoned docks. They even moved the Blue Peter Garden from London to Salford. Who would've thought! Now Salford includes this "Media City" and you can imagine the change such investment and commerce has brought the local residents. Alongside that, churches are growing and the unity movement is gathering even greater momentum. On a sabbatical visit I sat with Mark Ashcroft, Archdeacon of Manchester, and marvelled with him as we looked around the room of Gather leaders, at the potential breadth of the Christian unity movement in those cities.

The Spirit of unity is on the move and he is bringing churches and Christian agencies and charities together, to in turn bless the people of our communities.

Will you and yours cooperate or isolate? The choice is yours.

Endnotes
117. Silvoso, E, *That None Should Perish*, 1994, 123
118. John 17:21
119. For a full discussion of this, it is worth reading Alain Carion's *Apostolic Centres* – food for thought.

15

The Power of Unity and The Challenges of Denominations

"Take heed, then, often to come together to give thanks to God, and show forth His praise. For when you assemble frequently in the same place, the powers of Satan are destroyed, and the destruction at which he aims is prevented by the unity of your faith."

–Ignatius of Antioch

I am a little bit tentative to stop at this port on the journey and have a look around, because it is fraught with the intricate stories (mostly tragedies) that have stretched over centuries and resulted in what we find today. Apologies to Dr Meic Pearse, but I am not sure I paid sufficient attention in your wonderful Church History lectures! Nonetheless, we must consider the slightly broader perspective on this unity movement, namely the challenge of denominations.

I can remember the moment that my enthusiastic predecessor in the Watford AoG Church, Gordon Hickson, together with Graham Cracknell, encouraged church and charity leaders to take part in a foot-washing fraternal meeting. It was powerful, emotional, such that I can remember where I was, and who washed my feet. What can we do across denominations? We can wash one another's' feet. This is a beautiful symbol and expression of Christian unity, especially poignant for those who are called to lead. Because every leader is called to lead by serving. If you haven't washed someone's feet in a while, I recommend it. Maybe ask them first.

Where I am struggling in this whole inter-denominational matter is the unifying potential of communion. Let me explain: I am thinking about that same evening before Jesus was crucified. Having washed his disciples' feet (see above), our Lord then leads his followers, representatives of all who will follow after him, through the Passover meal. Powerfully, prophetically, he appropriates the bread and the wine to himself, to his impending sacrifice on the cross. He raises the special cup:

"This cup is the new covenant between God and his people in his blood."[120]

This is the most unifying ritual, the most holy sacrament that celebrates a new promise between our holy God and all those redeemed in Jesus name, by his blood. I know, this is a simple concept; it is meant to be. Every sinner-made-saint is invited to partake in this meal. It isn't a complex recipe and it unites believers in any language. It has for two thousand years.

The problem I have and will continue to work through, is deeply frustrating because it causes a problem between us. What am I talking about? Of course, I am referring to the Catholic/Protestant divide. Because of long-held, deep divisions in the Church I cannot (except through some special occasional dispensation) take communion in the Catholic church. Unless I go to confession; unless I make other pronouncements; unless I become a Catholic. I don't even want to pretend to tackle this issue in any depth, and I am not sure I would get very far if I tried. I am thrilled to read and hear of an increasing high-level cooperation between leaders of the Protestant, Eastern Orthodox and Catholic churches, and I pray for some way through in coming years.

The reason for bringing up the Lord's Table issue is because it is a powerful example of the Spirit's invitation to be united. It is meant to be not our table, but the Lord's! Jesus used the feast analogy so powerfully in one of his parables. Matthew and Luke both tell this story, though Matthew introduces a typically challenging end to it. In his version of the parable, Jesus talks of a king who prepares a wedding feast for his son. The guests receive the invitation but ignore it and go about their business. In angry response, the king extends the invitation to all and sundry, who indeed come and eat and celebrate; except one who is thrown out for unashamedly not bringing his best clothes to the banquet.[121]

Quite the story. Lots to unpack. I mention it here as a means of illustrating the central, pivotal, powerful nature of a meal where all are invited. This wedding banquet Jesus spoke of is, we understand, a tasty glimpse of the final Wedding Feast of Christ's return and the consummation of his kingdom on the earth. It also stirs within us a theme that for the first century audience was even more evocative than it is for us today, of a meal where people are invited to meet with God no matter who they are.

Communion. Literally, coming together with God; partaking, eye-to-eye; a love-feast. The Last Supper with his disciples was to become for every generation of believers since, the Lord's Supper with us and it is my conviction that it is a powerful uniter of people. Table fellowship, of course, was a central hallmark of the early Church:

"[The believers] worshiped together at the Temple each day, met in homes for the Lord's Supper, and shared their meals with great joy and generosity —all the while praising God and enjoying the goodwill of all the people. And each day the Lord added to their fellowship those who were being saved."[122]

This glowing picture of early Christian unity was put to the test in Acts 10 when Peter did the unthinkable: he broke bread with the Gentiles; even eating their unclean food. Who you eat with used to be a big deal and it still is. Had a secret dinner with the Queen, have you? If you had, how good would that feel? Shared your sandwich with a beggar on the street, have you?

Who we eat with matters. Around the Lord's Table I reckon we should be able to gather all those who call on his name, all those who believe in his death and resurrection. No repentant believer should be barred and it saddens me that denominational affiliations get in the way of this desire.

Through the Gather network mentioned earlier, I am beginning to hear of new ways of thinking in this whole area, and in some cases of Christian leaders from across the Catholic/ Protestant divide are meeting to share communion. This thrills me and shows us the way ahead. When we build high walls of denominational affiliation at the expense of God's ultimate aim (to unite all people under the headship of Christ), I believe our communities and our nation are missing out.

There is a picture here in my mind of one great Communion across the nation. In humility, celebrating rich diversity, it would see denominational affiliation relegated for the purposes of blessing our land. The essence of this inspired the 1980's "March for Jesus" movement and we proved we could (if willing) sing and wave banners together. Perhaps one day we could break bread together, the bread of the new covenant for all God's people? The power of one meal, as equals, no badges, showing a fractured world that division is not the end.

What matters in actuality is not who the Archbishop is, nor the Pope. It matters not whose branch of the Church we belong to. What matters most is the eternal King we are serving and there is only one of him.

The people of our nations are watching. They see political devolution and fragmented families, threatened unions and divided homes. They see Islamic fundamentalists and confused moderate Muslims. They are afraid to acknowledge differences and told we're all basically the same (when evidently the opposite is true). Some have been looking to the Church in recent years and what have they seen? Factions and petty divisions? Actually, I think they will begin to see something new happening. I believe we will show a united Church in our land laying down yesterday's arrogances and picking up invitations to a great and glorious feast. With low walls between denominations as well as their local expressions, we will be heading into the streets with these invites, telling people about the banquet of grace, where Jesus himself can be seen at the head of his table.

Endnotes
120. Luke 22:20
121. See Matthew 22:1-14
122. Acts 2:46-47

16
One Hope:
The Unity of Heaven

"Aim at heaven and you will get earth thrown in.
Aim at earth and you get neither.."
–C. S. Lewis

So we find ourselves reaching the beginning. It's the end of the book, but the new beginning of eternity (if you catch my drift). We find ourselves (from every tribe and tongue and nation), around that great banqueting table of the Lamb, taking part in the celebratory feast of all time.

It is a glorious sight, though even with John's help we struggle to picture it clearly. I guess we're meant to savour its potential:

"All glory to [Jesus Christ] who loves us and has freed us from our sins by shedding his blood for us. He has made us a Kingdom of priests for God his Father. All glory and power to him forever and ever! Amen. Look! He comes with the clouds of heaven. And everyone will see him— even those who pierced him. And all the nations of the world will mourn for him...

...I saw a vast crowd, too great to count, from every nation

and tribe and people and language, standing in front of the throne and before the Lamb. They were clothed in white robes and held palm branches in their hands. And they were shouting with a great roar, 'Salvation comes from our God who sits on the throne and from the Lamb!'" [123]

What a glorious picture. Jesus had entered the holy city of Jerusalem to the acclaim of a particular group of palm-waving Jews who proclaimed who he was. In John's glorious picture of heaven we see palm branches in the sanctified hands of cheering Christ-followers from every language, every tribe, even yours and mine. Abraham's promise fulfilled, diversity unified for the glory of God, not by the removal of difference, but the uniting of it.

The journey we have embarked on exploring unity amongst the people of Christ is incomplete, and we could have taken a different route, for sure. There are many talented thinkers further down the road than myself and there is so much more to learn about what unites us and how it all might work. In discussions with colleagues, I have often put forward the idea that our unity as churches in a locality is an end in itself. Others have told me we must be united with a mission; our unity must have an active purpose. I know what they mean (the boredom of inter-church meetings can be tiresome, I know) but I am not sure I agree. Unity in Christ is not a passive state of arrival, as much as the dynamic exploration of the very nature of God. And he is far from passive. It was said at the beginning of this that just as love is a destination and not just a means to it (God is love and he is our destination), so too unity is such an intrinsic expression of that love we must pursue it for its own sake.

Whenever we consider heaven we find ourselves caught in the now-and-not-yet of Christian life on earth. We are forgiven and in a right place before God, but we still need to prayerfully ask for forgiveness and work out our faith with fear and trembling. We must work out a salvation that is complete![124] In the same vein we can say in Christ that the Church is, ultimately united. All those who profess faith in him are united already in this one glorious hope. Yet today we are divided and need to maintain this unity in his family, at great cost and with concerted effort.

My prayer for you is that you will jointly accept this challenge with determination and openness to change, with humility before God and openness toward others. Including your spouse, and other team members, and people in your church. Some of those awkward "different" ones may well be seated next to you around that glistening gold table. Together we'll eat, drink and laugh, remembering the price Jesus paid to cleanse us all from our selfish sin.

This is our one hope. On that great day we'll worship as equals in God's eyes, adopted children in the Father's house, truly and forever united.

Endnotes

123. Revelation 1:5b-7, 7:9-10. I have stitched these together not to oversimplify the text or avoid due diligence regarding the context of these passages, but merely to illustrate the multi-faceted nature of heaven's harmony.
124. Philippians 2:12

Bibliography

The following is a list of the works that have played a substantive role in helping form my thoughts in preparation for this book:

Carion, A., 2013. *Apostolic Centers.* Colorado Springs: Arsenal Press.

Edwards, G., 1992. *The Tale of Three Kings:.* s.l.:Tyndale.

Foulkes, F., 1983. *The Epistle of Paul to the Ephesians: An Introduction and Commentary.* Leicester: Inter-Varsity Press.

Huffman, E. R. M., 2009. *Building a Missional City - Through Churches Working Together,* s.l.: (MA Dissertation, Birmingham Christian College).

Lincoln, A. T., 1990. *Word Biblical Commentary: Ephesians.* s.l.:Word, Incorporated.

Lloyd-Jones, D. M., 2003. *The Basis of Christian Unity.* s.l.:The Banner of Truth Trust.

Lloyd-Jones, D. M., 2006. *Christian Unity: An Exposition of Ephesians* 4:1-16. s.l.:The Banner of Truth Trust.

Maxwell, J. C., 2006. *The 21 Irrefutable Laws of Leadership.* s.l.:Maxwell Motivation.

Ortberg, J., 2003. *Everybody's Normal Till You Get to Know Them.* s.l.:Zondervan.

Page, N., 2012. *Kingdom of Fools: The Unlikely Rise of the Early Church.* s.l.:Hodder & Stoughton.

Ruibal, R., 2003. *Unity in the Spirit: Lessons from the Scriptures and Life in Cali, Columbia.* s.l.:TransformNations Media.

Sacks, J., 2003. *The Dignity of Difference.* Revised ed. London: Continuum.

Silvoso, E., n.d. *That None Should Perish.* 1994: Chosen Books.

Slipper, C., 2013. *5 Steps to Living Christian Unity.* New York: New City Press.

Snodgrass, K., 1996. *The NIV Application Commentary: Ephesians.* Grand Rapids: Zondervan.

Stott, J. R. W., 1991. *The Message of Ephesians: God's New Society.* Second ed. Leicester: Inter-Varsity Press.

Yancey, P., 2008. *Prayer: Does It Make Any Difference?.* Second Edition ed. s.l.:Hodder and Stoughton.